MW00814420

Deep Joy, Steep Challenge:
365 Poems On Parenting

by: Charles C.Finn

To Cathy
Things here guaranteed to
bring smiles and sighs

Charlie
September 2005

authorHOUSE™

1663 LIBERTY DRIVE, SUITE 200
BLOOMINGTON, INDIANA 47403
(800) 839-8640
WWW.AUTHORHOUSE.COM

© 2005 Charles C. Finn. All Rights Reserved.

No part of this book may be reproduced, stored in a retrieval system, or transmitted by any means without the written permission of the author.

First published by AuthorHouse 09/02/05

ISBN: 1-4208-7537-X (sc)

Printed in the United States of America
Bloomington, Indiana

This book is printed on acid-free paper.

For parents everywhere
called to arduous bliss.

Table of Contents

Foreword

Deep Joy, Steep Challenge witnesses to the arduous bliss of parenting a child, inviting other parents to remember their hundred good reasons to fret, their thousand good reasons to sing.

"What is most personal is most universal." The poems that follow, one for each day of the year, will test this paradoxical assertion. The reflections in them, cast in easily readable poetic form, are decidedly personal—stemming from actual experiences with our daughter and son—yet the themes struck are far from unique. While I write on many subjects, often it's the poems about my children that especially strike a chord in people, most never having met them.

Since our children were pre-adolescent at the time, these reflections relate only to early and middle childhood. Our hope, like that of parents everywhere, is that the foundation we were laying these early years would provide sufficient grounding in adolescence for burgeoning identity and eventual flight.

Exacting, exasperating, exhausting, rich, awe-inspiring, transforming—all are accurate partial descriptions of the high calling of parenthood, a calling from the Universe to marvel before its evolution reenacted, a calling from the Earth to nurture and embolden the children she entrusts, calls eliciting from parents all the intelligence, heart, imagination and spirit they can muster that they might mold nothing less than the future.

Preparation

Look In Their Eyes And See

Today is ageless,
for a man is choosing his woman
and a woman is choosing her man.
What is this thing called marriage?
Two people, unique to each other in all the world, now declare it to
    all the world,
sing it from the rooftops,
make public their proclamation of love.
"This is our moment!" they exclaim to those gathered and held most
    dear.
"Come rejoice with us and wish us fair journey."
Then tears and laughter,
then celebration sweetens the air.
Ah, how playfully creative is the spirit of Earth, the spirit of life,
how enamored of this simple theme.
This drama unfolding here
is an endearingly disguised reenactment of the cosmic drama!
Through this individual man and woman,
fleshed at a precise point in time,
the shining Earth creates anew the primordial once-upon-a-time,
the archetypal marriage of heaven and Earth,
of yang and yin,
of man and woman.
This is the solemn moment, the sacred moment,
the resplendent mystic point where marriages of all ages intersect
    and are one.
Look in their eyes and see: in their exultation, the Earth exults!
Today is ageless,
for a man is choosing his woman
and a woman is choosing her man.

June 1976

3

Shimmering Jewel

In early morning featherbed warmth
when you curl up on top of me and drowsily we whisper our love,
a man-fullness fills me
and my mind at peace ranges far.
In that pristine stillness
when the open windows spread diamonds all around us
of singing birds and gathering light,
I thank the Heart of Life, my Penny,
for the shimmering jewel of you.
Since our day in May under our magic tree
four circlings of the seasons have brought us
beyond our hopes but not our dreams
to Cor Mundi, the Heart of the World.
A man-fullness fills me
and my mind at peace ranges far.

May 21, 1981

Five Sweet And Swirling Years

It's been five sweet and swirling years
since big stones witnessed a big question
and wondrously you did say yes.
What a journey that whirled us into—
sapphires dancing around a diamond,
Jamaican winter escape,
May vows under a linden,
blooming apartment on Columbia,
night walks on Lake's edge,
working together at the Institute,
following mayonnaise to meaning,
Sunday sharings with Kevin and Vicki and Jim and Winnie,
and then, after a Chicago farewell and traveling through a Europe
    of wonders,
staying true to our search till finding in the mountains of Virginia
the land of our dreams and the heart of our world.
If I had it to do over, my Penny,
stoned or not I'd ask you anew
to walk with me wherever destiny leads.
And though we've lived what feels a lifetime already,
there's a road ahead to test us with its rigors
and bless us with its joys.
Say yes to me again, my love,
as we make ready, destiny willing,
for the diamond children coming.

August 18, 1981

Diamond Child Coming

Six Novembers ago
in a bustling Mexican restaurant on the shore of a northern sea
two destinies—
in sweet conspiracy with candles and music and wine—
interlaced,
and the ancient fire-drama was kindled anew.
Love, that sent wheeling the atoms and stars
and flowered an orbiting rock into life,
that cultivated across the ages human soaring minds and cherishing
     hearts,
this very Love that impassions the whole sweep of a universe
unfolds once again the splendor and the mystery
first in a November falling in love
and now in the silent magnitude of a diamond child that is coming.
The loving cosmos bows down
to the rebirth of fire
in the Heart of the World.

September 1981

Good God, I'm On The Brink

Father—
strong, solid, able to be trusted;
tender, protecting, able to be loved;
less a metaphor for the mystery of God's loving
than the enfleshed reality of God's loving.
Good God, I'm on the brink
not only of an archetypal reenactment
but of an absolute new venturing
of the fathering-forth Spirit of the universe!

August 1984

Gardeners Dreaming

Tiny Korean flower,
half an Earth away in a fertile mountain valley our garden awaits
    you.
After the shock of transplanting,
may your tender roots sink into our eager soil
and find here sufficient warmth and nourishment to grow into a
    beautiful blossoming.
This is our prayer for you,
infinite one in newest disguise,
you who will shape our lives as profoundly as we will yours.
May you find here the love of which you are worthy,
April Amanda of our dreaming.

January 1985

Search Your Origin And Find Love

Some day when you search your origin, my daughter,
wondering if you were loved,
know that as soon as we saw your picture
and were told you could be ours if we wanted,
you became in that moment our daughter.
Instantly we loved you,
instantly a YES flooded out of us—
tears from your mother's eyes, overflowing from your father's
    heart.
You are April, green Earth singing in springtime with flowers in
    her hair.
You are Amanda, worthy to be loved,
of such beauty and worth that knowing you will be loving you.
You are Daughter of the Sun, Earthchild loved beyond galaxies of
    imagining
by the Presence behind all love.
April Amanda Daughter of the Sun,
search your origin and find love.

January 1985

And she said yes!

Daughter

For April's Welcoming Celebration

For a word-lover, April, your father is at a loss to string a few
to make you his wish.
Everything that life has taught me
wants to leap straight from my heart to yours,
but it doesn't work that way.
You have to come to your own learnings,
find and be true to your own star.
What I do wish you, bright daughter of my life,
is open eyes and an open heart.
I have a gigantic trust that this mystical treasure of a universe,
including the glittering jewel we sail around the sun on,
is alive with such a loving Presence
that we only need to be open to it to be united with it.
You too are part of this Grand Communion, April,
but there will be times ahead for you of thunder and darkness
when doubt can't see it,
fear will flee it.
Keep open, Daughter of the Sun.
Listen to your Earth-heart, discover what makes it sing,
then make your life follow.
I pray your mother and I build under you a strong foundation
and then get out of the way—
a steady bow so that the arrow can fly far.
While we'd like to shield you from pain we know we can't,
for one of the deepest mysteries has it
that without pain we can't become healers of each other or the
Earth.
Keep open, April with the sun and moon within,
your eyes and your heart.

April 14, 1985

A Universe Expanding

My daughter is discovering words—
up to 6 or 7 clear and distinct ones.
She's beginning to make *connections*.
She sees something and knows the right word for it,
and when she speaks it and is praised,
how proud she is of her fine accomplishment,
how she glows with it.
"Ball."
"Yes, that's a ball, April, good for you! Now go get it and bring it
    to Daddy."
And she gets it and brings it to me,
and I congratulate her again and she glows again.
Can you imagine how good it must feel to be 14 months young
and given a hurrah by the most important people in your world?
You'd have to want to hug yourself it'd feel so good.
Then it's on to "dog" or "book"
or to who knows what new connection next?
The universe is expanding, we are told—
in my daughter I can see it!

August 1985

What A Decade, Girl

How amazing, my Penny,
to think of the places we've traveled to,
the people we've loved,
the growing we've done.
And though it feels a lifetime it's just beginning
for now incredibly there's the flower of our April—
beautiful beyond description,
sharp as a tack,
coming more each day into her own bright spirit,
entrusted by Life to our keeping and guiding.
How she multiplies a thousand-fold our previous joy,
she towards whom we've been ripening
after ripening towards each other.
I love you, April's mother and Charlie's partner for life.
November of 75 to November of 85—
what a decade, girl.

November 1985

Always Woman Loved

Sapphires engaged in a dance around a diamond,
    wildflowers afloat in a garden of their own,
petunias cascading from the porch in summer,
    trees bending in pleasure with apple and peach treasure,
horses dignified just standing but in motion majestic!—
    images dear to a woman loved
whose heart knows darkness but holds to light,
    knows aching from loving but keeps loving.
Warrioress resolute,
    mother resourceful,
always woman loved.
    Penny.

May 1986

Oh The Comfort To Them Both

In the shadows
a father stands outside his little girl's bedroom and listens.
She had begun to stir,
to cry a little in her sleep,
and he has come.
If she eases back down he'll leave her be, entrusting her to the
    night.
But if she keeps stirring he's ready to enter.
It may be only to cover her with a blanket so she'll feel warm and
    snug,
or to get her some water,
or to rock her for comfort if it's a tummy ache
or the thunder
or a bad dream.
Oh the comfort to them both when deep in the night
a father holds in his arms his little girl
and soothes her to sleep.

September 1986

No Greater Poignancy

After a sick child recovers,
it's amusing to recall the extremities of worry the parents were
carried to.
And if they're first parents, well, it's to be expected.
Veterans smile at such overreactions, but kindly, for they
remember.
But before the recovery, the dread is as real as a stab is real.
When her temperature is rising
and screams rip away every parental defense
and everything done that the doctor said to do quells neither fever
nor pain,
and when the voice over the phone says bring her to the ER right
away,
the parent's heart can't help but be seized with a fear
that maybe everything *won't* be OK.
We read the newspaper,
we watch TV—
sometimes the worst does happen.
When the car hurtles through the night,
shadows descend and fear clutches.
Regardless the presence or absence of a theology, there escapes from
the parent's heart an involuntary cry.
Please let her be OK.
Please God, please Life, let her stop hurting and be OK.
There's no greater poignancy
than differential cries from child and parents
hurtling towards a hospital deep in the night.

November 1986

I Can't See My Book

What does a grown man (answering proudest to "Daddy") do
when he turns off a Mickey Mouse desk light
only to hear his little girl, age 2, eyes long shut in sleep,
manage a hazy protest, "I can't see my book, I can't see"?
Why, he turns it back on, of course.
Who needs a squabble in the wee sweet hours of a bright new year?

January 1987

Without Aiming

A 2-year-old without aiming
    lives the mystic's aim:
what is before her absorbs her.
    Grown accustomed to miracles my eyes see beyond them
until the hand of my daughter
    leads me back to the infinity of wonder.

January 1987

The Span Of A Rainbow

A grandfather for a companion
is a marvelous treat for a girl of 2,
and her hand in his
inexpressibly refreshes his soul.
A seeming unbridgeable gap in years
becomes but the span of a rainbow
when innocence perches on wisdom's lap
or when both go out for an earnest walk
hunting pebbles or puddles or who knows what
and maybe inviting a fox back to lunch
(or a unicorn if they're lucky).

January 1987

An Amazing Thing About Adoption

There's an amazing thing about adoption.
Before Penny and I embarked upon the journey,
we figured it would be fine and good but not quite the same.
We'd become a family and all
and grow to love our adopted children deeply,
but surely something would have to be missing.
It stood to reason.
Implicit here was our very real grieving.
For seeming essential it's a dream difficult to let go of—
    bringing your own children into being.
But then the amazing thing only fathomed by other
    adoptive parents.
We thank God for our previous sorrow.
We thank God we were unable to have a natural child
for then we wouldn't have known our April.
We wanted her,
we chose her,
we now love her with such fierce tenderness
that not to have had her would have been the real loss.
Just a father jabbering about his daughter
for not knowing how else to sing

February 1987

Long Live Rituals

Bedtime rituals can get quite intricate.
None of this story, kiss, and goodnight simplicity,
not for us anyway.
Those three elements are present, of course, but there's much
  besides.
It really starts with jammies and brushing teeth,
each of which has a mini-ritual of its own.
Let me hasten to say that this whole elaborate ritual
is not at all tedious or unpleasant.
Once it has been established, it becomes a comfortable-because-
  anticipated routine,
not to mention a time for impish fun
when games of mini-resistance peek around the corner.
Which is not to deny occasional storms—
what better way to vent frustration than by defying longstanding
  ritual?
But ritual time is usually not conflict time.
It's ease down time, security time, time to squawk a little at having
  to give up the day,
but pretty soon the fatigue that's been building catches up.
After diaper and jammies are in order and teeth can be heard
  singing,
it's time for the round of goodnights.
First it's out to the porch to tell the stars goodnight (a few by name)
and the moon and Evening Star if we're lucky
and the mountain backlit by the city.
Then it's night-night to each of our six animals
sprawled in contented oblivion on cushions or woodfloor.
And finally hugs and kisses to Grandfather and Mommy.
But that only gets us to the bedroom.
Like I say, rituals can get intricate.
Once in the room it's pick-out-a-book time
which calls for earnest perusal of the bookshelf—
who can argue that it's not important to get just the right one?
Then it's to the rocker for our reading followed by a little singing

(three songs max supposedly, but Daddy has been known to relax
    the limit on occasion).
We end this segment of the ritual with an impromptu prayer of
    thanks for the day.
Then after turning on all by herself the humidifier, it's into the crib.
But we're not finished yet.
We need a little Vicks on our chest
and guess who must unscrew the lid all by herself?
Then it's big hug time
and soft kiss on cheek
and arranging the blanket just so (the new-new one, not the heavy
    one or the rainbow one).
We also have to check to make sure a few books are on hand (you
    never know when sleep just won't come).
About this time I'm reminded that bedtime rituals make a girl of 2
    and a half terribly thirsty,
so it's Daddy off to get a glass of water (now you know why she's
    still in a diaper).
After thirst has been slaked (a bunny sip usually does it),
we're running out of legitimate stalling tactics,
but Daddy still has to wind up the rotating Easter bunny musical egg
    given by Grandmother last spring.
I mean, who can argue with a little bedtime music?
Our ritual is drawing to a close.
After a final hug (it seems the first one lacked a little something),
I tell her for the final time how much Mommy and Daddy love her
and make my exit.
Not long thereafter predictably comes a call for Daddy.
It seems he forgot something important along the way
or if not then we're maybe thirsty again or need another little hug.
At which point innocent urchin is duly informed that this is it.
Daddy's not coming back again however steadfastly or vociferously
    she may plead.
She assures me she'll not call me back.
She knows she's stretched things as far as they can go and it still be
    fun.
It has indeed been a gentle, endearing kind of fun.

"Goodnight, sweetheart. How much does Daddy love you?"
"Soooooo much" as she stretches out her arms to infinity.
End of ritual.
When people espouse eliminating ritual from religious worship,
they're crazy.

February 1987

Pep Talk

Being tested by a 2-year-old can grind you down.
When screams shift from rage to pleading,
defenses around a father's heart weaken.
Sobbing, plaintive calls to Daddy feel like knives.
What will this do to her trust in the world
if she calls and her Daddy won't come?
Get hold of yourself, Daddy.
If she gets to blow people away with her storms,
who's to protect her against herself?
What this is *about* is trust—
that Daddy's word means something,
that it can't be bought off by a storm or a pleading.
Some poems serve as pep talks
to stand up to a test.

February 1987

If A Child, Why Not A Cosmos?

How sad that evolution is a fighting word instead of a wonder word.
Look at a child.
Reductionists keep looking back, reduce present to past,
find nothing really new under the sun.
But what is an infant crawling, then walking, then incomprehensibly
    talking,
if not bodymind evolving,
fresh spirit miraculously evolving?
Each new whole—greater than the sum of its preceding parts—
keeps advancing with imperceptible unfolding
or with rare prodigious leaps.
Is an infant's astounding metamorphosis into an adult human being
    so unlike Earth's from matter to life, life to mind, mind to
    spirit?
If a child so obviously evolves, why not a cosmos?
And if indeed tomorrow brings to us and in us something
    breathtakingly new under the sun,
is this less a bang than the big one,
less a day of creation than the first?
How ennobling to participate in an evolving universe, with
    imperceptible unfolding or rare prodigious leaps.
Ah, what a wonder word is evolution!

February 1987

Dumbo Planting A Seed

My daughter's fascination with *Dumbo* continues—
she's seen it dozens of times and keeps wanting more.
The seed it may be planting in her
is a rich one indeed.
Here's this pitiable creature,
derided for big ears which make him seem good for nothing,
who discovers magic in the form of a feather that apparently allows
    him to fly
only to come close to crashing when said feather wafts away
before discovering, thanks to his trusty mouse guide, the deepest
    secret:
the very thing he was derided for
was the means by which he could fly!
I can't keep from my girl of 2
derision and disillusionment in the years ahead,
but I can pray she stay open to guides along the way
reminding her that aspects of herself she may least appreciate
may be the magic by which she can honest-to-God fly.

March 1987

Sounds I Love

Sounds I love:
rain,
surf breaking,
wind at night,
woodstove fire,
waterfall,
mockingbird,
thunder,
birds at dawn,
snow falling,
breathing,
"Daddy."

March 1987

Grand Introduction

My daughter is almost 3.
When a body reaches upward (like a flower in spring),
when a mind opens bright to a world of light,
when a personality deepens daily into endearing singularity,
how can one disbelieve in miracles?
Parenthood from afar may seem tedious and constricting,
but up close it catches your breath,
draws on every one of your powers.
To be a father or a mother is a grand introduction
to a universe that flowers!

March 1987

Kitty Hawk

April was up early this morning.
You'd think knowing I was on early duty
I'd have sense enough not to stay up late,
but who thinks sense with surf pounding,
with poems waiting to be delivered?
Happily she was up for about as much action as I was
so we had a drowsy-with-dreaming hour,
magical hour if ever one was,
with her snuggling in my arms drinking juice, sinking back into
    sleep's trusting,
and me listening in turn to the beating against the shore and the
    breathing against my chest,
musing as I rocked on a destiny rich
bringing gifts such as these.

April 1987

Cracking The Code

At not quite 3 April has yet to crack the code.
The mystic symbols are still to her
what Viking runes are to most of us—
incomprehensible markings.
But the threshold day is not far distant
when she'll be able to name them and sing them and herself weave
    them into new meanings
for being able to *decipher* them.
What an awakening awaits her when runes called letters,
juxtaposed as if by chance,
will join hands beyond her present imagining
in a luminous dance!

April 1987

From Chaos To Cosmos

The morning begins in chaos
with every room in disarray, some close to disaster.
Penny's off to work and there I am faced with it—
top priority a child to attend to
but also a gargantuan mess to make disappear.
It can most certainly be a drag
particularly if attention to detail is not your strong suit,
ah, but it can also be a saga,
an epic to equal that of Gilgamesh, Odysseus or Arthur,
or of God the Father creating nothing less from chaos than cosmos!
Housework may seem a demeaning drudgery,
but if family's pride and comfort and health are at stake,
what a noble endeavor!
Of course, maintaining the energy of creation is fatiguing
but "Fiat lux!" can be each room's command,
and after patient laboring returns it to order
comes the richly satisfying pausing
to see that it is good!

April 1987

Of All The Songs That Speak To Her

Listen to "The Rose" if you would know her,
if you would learn of her essential spirit,
her capacity for compassion,
her faith in love,
her understanding born of living through darkness
that darkness is not final.
Of all the songs that speak to Penny,
none speaks more deeply than "The Rose."

April 1987

God Talking

Taking a break from my writing,
I stopped at two doors to hear God talking.
Penny was on the phone with a suicidal vet,
guiding him through jungle darkness,
urging him to keep clinging.
Then to April's room to overhear a nasty troll,
"WHO'S THAT TRIP-TRAPPING ON MY BRIDGE?"
Somehow the juxtaposition in the evening quiet
of those two voices from those two rooms
confirms for me the power and preciousness of existence
and stabs me with a joy I can only stammer.
No question it was God I heard talking.

April 1987

Graybear

Waking from sleep April noticed me gazing (as fathers are wont to
    do)
and, reaching out a hand, simply said "Graybear."
I nestled her teddy between her shoulder and cheek
and like that she was back asleep.
How important to her and precious to me her Graybear.
May each of us have had a time of trust
with one of Graybear's kind.

April 1987

No Ordinary Hole

My daughter and I checked out a hole in the hillside.
We were thinking fox den
(having just read *The Fox And The Hound*)
but after seeing the dogs chase a rabbit
suddenly we understood.
We had stumbled upon the very home in the Earth
where the Easter Bunny himself must be catching a snooze
before next week hiding the eggs of the world.
Let me tell you, there was reverence in our whisper
as we wished him soft sleep and sweet dream
before hopping to it.

April 1987

Charles C. Finn

Sometimes Not By The Book

Sometimes you don't go by the book.
April got scared by a huge fly tonight.
She was winding towards sleep when she heard the buzzing
and thought it was a wasp that might hurt her.
When I came in she was literally trembling.
Despite the fly's prompt demise, she couldn't be calmed,
pleading not to go back to her bed but to sleep with mommy and
    daddy.
We know what the book says,
but there's a difference between manipulation and dread.
Tonight we chose to ignore the book
and soothe our girl's fear instead.

April 1987

38

No More Disappointment Crap

Thanks to feedback from Penny,
I cringed to see something tonight but it led to a resolve.
When April disobeys, I'd been saying "that disappoints me."
What Penny helped me see is "disappointment" is loaded—
disguises anger,
throws April guilt for "making" me disappointed,
for letting me down.
Ouch!
But I see it now and can change.
I can be straighter with my anger,
more specific about cause and desired change.
No more disappointment crap
to burden girl not yet 3.

April 1987

Just The Right Brother

This is a pivotal time.
My wife and I soon will make a decision
that will alter all that follows.
A door was suddenly shut on us.
The Korean infant we were hoping to adopt,
April's brother-to-be from the land of her birth,
is not to be.
My age is the issue, tighter laws have been set.
There's a terrible sinking in the heart when a dream suddenly dies,
when a heart's long preparing feels suddenly in vain.
So now we begin entertaining other possibilities, exploring other
     avenues.
Difficult questions are put to us—
will you take an older child,
a child with special needs,
a bi-racial child,
a foreign child?
You never know how you'll answer
until crunch-time hits and you have to.
But I remember our initial dream of a Taiwanese child that also
     wasn't to be,
and today we look at April with tears in our eyes
thanking God for the dream that was dashed.
So who knows?
Maybe April will have an Indian brother
or a Filipino or Chinese brother
or a black brother.
What's important is she will have a brother
who, trust has it, will be just the right brother in all the world.

April 1987

40

Steeped With Caring

Hers is a heart attuned to nurturing—
plants that they may breathe beauty,
animals that they may know gentleness and affection,
children that they may blossom under the sun of her cherishing,
crusty veterans that they may believe again in themselves and in
    life.
Past her mind sharp with ten thousand learnings
is her heart steeped with caring.
I write here of my life's partner, my child's mother—
catch hint of my joy!

May 1987

Best Friends

April told me in emphatic 2-year-old fashion
as we drove home today from a round of errands,
"Grandfather is not my friend, he's my *best* friend."
I couldn't wait to tell Milton and make his day.
I hope I make it to grandfatherhood some day.
Life I trust will still feel full if I don't,
but I intuit deeply the power and tenderness of this bond
overarching a generation like a rainbow.
April would miss something vital and precious
were here grandfather not our guest these months.
While she's not likely to remember back to 2,
you can't convince me his impact on her won't be felt across her
    lifetime,
and not only his impact on her.
I have to believe his declining years
have become a little less declining thanks to her.
What friends to each other they have become—
oops, I mean *best* friends.

May 1987

Precious

My daughter is precious.
The word, through overuse, has lost its sapphire sparkle, its infinity
    of tenderness,
but I'll chance it anyway.
She just stumbled out to the living room to give me a hug.
She doesn't usually stir once she's down for the night,
but I guess the music was a little loud.
Those eyes even if sleepy,
those arms trusting around me.
A drink of juice was a very good idea
and soon it was time to be carried by daddy back to bed
for a final tuck-in and kiss.
Not only are children precious,
we are precious when we allow them to reach us,
to penetrate our armor,
to break through the encrustations of time.
Precious may sound trite and sentimental,
but not to the knowing heart.

May 1987

An Awesome Thing Is Foreign Adoption

Beginning the process of adopting a Chinese boy,
somewhere around 2 years old,
brings home the crashing realization
that half a world away in a Hong Kong orphanage
our son, some day to find his home in Virginia,
is already *alive.*
Think of the odds against our even meeting, much less becoming
    family.
An awesome thing is foreign adoption—
fits Earth into the palm of a hand,
reveals a single family, rainbow family,
widens the soul for all its blessings and testings,
enlarges destiny's mind-numbing heart-thrilling mystery.
We may never know the delivery room ecstasy,
but we'll have an airport ecstasy of our own.
I can't get over that our son,
some day to fly through the sky to our arms,
now in Hong Kong at this exact moment is alive!

May 1987

Grieving Already Underway

Penny was telling April in the car today
that when her baby brother comes
he'll have the same parents as she.
With a comprehending flash of displeasure,
emphatically she said *no*.
You can take sharing just too far—
toys and books and animals, maybe,
but no way mommy and daddy too.
Amusing her spontaneity but real her dismay,
softening our hearts with a resolution
to comfort and reassure her as best we can
through grieving already underway.

May 1987

45

When Haven Turns Cage

The move from crib to bed may seem no big deal
until you imagine yourself back into remembering.
It's safer in the crib,
snugger with animals stacked around,
more comforting for all the loving there,
but the time comes when it's plain too confining.
There are new risks, to be sure, but, ah, the new freedom
when you can get up to read when sleep is slow coming,
make it to the bathroom all by yourself,
paddle in to mommy and daddy for earnest communications
    tomorrow can't wait for.
Almost equal to my joy at her literal leap into freedom
is my sadness at this confirmation that my infant is no longer.
Parenthood is a trip, let me tell you.

May 1987

The Endearment Of 3

April informed me this evening
that when she gets bigger and bigger
she'll have her kittens in the woods just like Kitty Cat.
I assured her she can have her kittens anywhere she wants.
The endearment of 3.

June 1987

Noble Calling

"The hand that rocks the cradle rules the world."
Now I understand.
Caretakers of small children have the noble calling
of affecting the future by grounding human life
in protection, nurturance and delight—
the wherewithal for eventual flight.
Self-sacrifice is the price,
but the recompense, beyond service to today,
is shaping no less extravagant immensity
than tomorrow!

June 1987

Tall Order, Bold Promise

These are the fierce days of setting and sticking to limits,
no matter the assault ensuing.
April skipped the terrible two's only to land in the terrible three's.
Of course she tests the limits.
How else test power, emphatically feel being?
How else taste the joy of self-assertion, of defiant negation,
without which life overwhelms?
But needing to come into self-empowerment
need not mean coming into anarchy.
If parents aren't united as to limits and consequences,
their child will seem the winner but be the loser,
will reap terror and confusion.
But if consequences include flesh or spirit bruising,
how will the child not presume harshness from the world
and only bide time until big enough to return the infliction?
A tall order for parents
simultaneous with a bold promise:
talk often with each other
in order to stand together kindly but firmly,
to withstand assault together firmly but kindly,
and be confident that what you are cultivating
is a garden your child can play in,
that what you are painstakingly building
is a foundation your child can stand on.
Vigorous, rigorous, but essential are the terrible two's—
or is it the terrible three's?

July 1987

Charles C. Finn

Think Of Our Gift

We have a Korean daughter
and soon will have a Chinese son.
Think of our gift.
Children from the other side of Earth
here in our house will live and grow.
Here glittering diversity will sparkle into unity!
We all give lip-service to the family of man,
but how rare the stupendous privilege of experiencing one's
    own house
turned into a planetary home.
Think of our gift.

July 1987

Cincinnati Zoo

A snow leopard pausing long between cool lappings,
a baby hippo and elephant going at it in play,
unforgettable jaguar eyes but inches away,
the gorgeous fierce whiteness of a tiger stalking,
a bald eagle motionless but still majestic,
the first camel ride in her life for a 3-year-old—
the trip to the Cincinnati zoo
impacted more than the 3-year-old.

July 1987

Counselor Turned Sandbox Father

To be a counselor and simultaneously a father
makes for exquisite discoveries.
I have to believe Freud would have been less morose about the human
    condition
if theorizing in his study about toddlers
had yielded more often to playing with them in the sandbox.
This is an enthusiastic endorsement, by the way, of primary care-
    giving by fathers,
of the rich maternal secrets housedaddies discover
hidden in their own being.
Psychiatric professionals bound still to Freud
hold that all the good you see in children—
magical curiosity, energetic glee, even budding loving—
is but the creative channeling of a convulsion within.
Counselor turned sandbox father can't help but see deeper.
This poem proves nothing.
It's a pure cry of joy from the heart of a father
in the process of discovering no less glory than God
lighting up his child from within.
Sublimation, I'll not deny it,
but decidedly something more.

August 1987

I Love That Bower

Back from my night walk I hear April calling,
wondering where I've been.
Being in bed for a big girl of 3
is no guarantee of being asleep.
When I answer, "to our secret bower," pleasure leaps to
    her face.
She then recounts with pride how she and daddy removed
    weeds and leveled dirt,
brought in chairs to sit on,
and then named all the trees surrounding.
With big round eyes she summed it up, "I love that secret
    bower."
With that we hugged a golden hug that shared a golden
    secret
and then kissed goodnight.

August 1987

That Makes A Marriage Work

Who says you have to go shopping to give a gift.
Penny today gave me an afternoon,
took April swimming to allow me time of my own.
This is the kind of gift that makes a marriage work—
small, but not really,
sheer out of the blue kindness,
no shopping necessary.

August 1987

Parents, Not Drill Sergeants

The wisest thing I learned from a book on childrearing
was a tip to let your child win an occasional skirmish.
When it comes to the major battles, the parents must not bend—
not to break spirit (cherished even when checked)
but to provide security,
to establish firm enough parameters for the child to count on.
But parents need to yield sometimes if not to become
    drill sergeants.
Battles need parents to hold sway,
but occasional skirmishes need to go the other way.

August 1987

Humping Along

It's fun to reminisce with a 3-year-old
about when she was just a little kid.
April and I went to get the mail today,
a half mile walk with a couple of steep climbs.
Lazy Bones insisted on riding Camel,
and while Camel disgruntled (as self-respecting camels do)
Lazy Bones not surprisingly prevailed.
And what we reminisced about while humping along
was how fun it used to be.
Through infancy and wobbly toddlerhood,
such a jaunt with her babbling in my backpack was a daily ritual.
Today we giggled to remember—
she a burgeoning 3,
me past that a tad but still holding my own
carrying Lazy Bones and humping along.

August 1987

Two Mistakes

Teenage girl to mischievous little boy near April and me in the
     store:
"You're mean! Why can't you be like that nice little girl?"
Two mistakes.
You don't label a young person mean, even in jest,
without risk it will linger,
will become a self-judgment.
And you don't, even in praise, say "nice little girl"
within earshot of a big girl of 3.

August 1987

If You Call, I Will Come

I just had the sweetest conversation with April upon
    returning from my walk.
Perched in bed with animals affectionately strewn,
she asked if I had a good walk and where did I go?
(I learned later from Penny she had cried after me,
running out to the porch calling "Daddy!")
So I tell her about my walk to the hill where we go
    sometimes,
where the dogwood and wild cherry stand sentinel,
and about flashes lighting up the sky beyond the mountains
announcing thunder soon coming.
She informed me after earnestly listening
that she's glad the storm will water the flowers and trees
but if it's a daddy thunder instead of a mommy or baby one,
she may get scared and call "Daddy!"
Tucking her and her animals in,
I assure her with a nuzzle and a squeeze,
"If you call, little one, I will come."

August 1987

Retrieve The Blank Screen

You can so lavish affection on your first child,
be so enamored of all her ways,
that waiting for number two brings gathering fear
that he'll always suffer for never measuring up,
until you're rescued by the remembrance
that just as it was against expectation's blank screen
that she blossomed into such original vitality,
so your greatest gift now to him
will be to retrieve the blank screen.

September 1987

Good For You

I heard a thud last night from April's room
and hastened to cradle her up gently from the floor
    back to the center of her bed.
Barely awakening from it all,
she managed the sweetest mumble in my direction,
    "Good for you."
How nice to be congratulated by your kid for doing just the right
    thing.
Without a doubt parents shape their children's behavior,
but less, I suspect, than vice versa.

September 1987

A Lift From A Letter

April's letter to Mommy
earnestly dictated to Daddy through tears:
"I want my Mommy.
I'm crying because Daddy mopped the bathroom floor and I didn't
    want him to.
Daddy's hair is in his face but I fixed it.
Daddy and I are going to visit our neighbors and invite them to our
    party.
I want my Mommy.
Please come home soon as you can. Love, April"
Reading it,
Mommy's heart at the end of a ragged day
suddenly lifted.

September 1987

Delicious

April's at that delicious stage
where, giggling, she covers her eyes and says, "You can't see me."
Hide and seek,
monster chase,
surprise bundle under the towels—
attentiveness, drama, abandon, glee.
The Kingdom of heaven and children are inseparable.
Her invisible companions keep changing—
still Jon-Michel in North Carolina
but increasingly Mandy from Day School
and now (for some very good reason) Greedy Smurf.
Delicious.

September 1987

Swimming In The Sea Of It

Adoptive parents maybe have an edge,
accept from the outset the dimension in the child of mystery, utter
    and inaccessible,
heightening respect for difference,
reverence before the unknown.
Biological parents, facts of birth being known,
might assume they know their child and skim over the mystery.
Adoptive parents swim in the sea of it.

September 1987

All Over Again New

Child number two on the way has impossible footsteps to follow,
so parents be advised:
scrap all expectations,
it'll all over again be new, meaning absolutely different.
Trying to fit number two into the mold of number one
mutilates number two.
Allowing, instead, for the infinity of God's masks,
welcome beneath disguise of number two
brand new gift and bold new challenge.

September 1987

Spice Added To My Life

I'm married to a wizardress—
not that she's sinister or far out,
in fact she's so down-to-Earth fresh and real you'd never suspect her
    craft,
her obedience to nameless That which leads,
her attunement to the universe's secret unfoldings.
In Tolkein's *The Hobbit* and his ensuing trilogy,
one glories to meet the wizard Gandalf
without whom unlikely heroes like Bilbo and Frodo
never would have made it to the Dark Tower and back,
never would have journeyed to begin with.
Think of the spice that's been added to my life
to discover in my wife a Gandalf!

September 1987

Elfin Zen Master

When I let all April teaches us sink in (and she's only 3)
I realize she's literally a guru to us,
an elfin Zen master wise in innocence,
insistent with spontaneity about the kingdom at hand.

September 1987

Bubbling Out Unbidden

I know altruism can only flower later,
but my daughter's genuinely generous heart
that bubbles out unbidden at the seasoned age of 3
leads me to intuit with a measure of certainty
that she'll come some day to know
with all the joy and pain of it
wide loving.

October 1987

Fruit Cottontail

"Fruit cottontail"—
April's answer when I asked what her snack was today.
After a hearty laugh on her fine invention,
I got to thinking if I were into selling desserts
I couldn't miss with Fruit Cottontail.
Add to fruit cocktail plenty of miniature marshmallows,
picture a cute bunny on the can with marshmallow tailpuff,
and every small kid would beg parents to buy some.
I have it on good authority that parents of the very young
quite often do as they're told.

October 1987

Nothing Touches Like Kindness

A couple knowing of our wait for a child from China—
themselves having endured the same wait—
made us a tape of Chinese phrases
so that amidst our son's initial bewilderment
he might at least have the ground of familiar sounds to stand on.
Knowing the gift's value they gave it.
Nothing touches like kindness.

October 1987

Noble Beings

Fairy tales, I muse as I read to April, are hard on wolves.
First it was *The Three Pigs* and *Little Red Riding Hood.*
Then came *Peter and the Wolf* and *The Wolf and the Seven Kids.*
Now it's *Aesop's Fables* chiming in
about the menacing, villainous wolf.
Such a consistently bad press
for such an admirable animal when the facts are known.
Thank goodness for *Never Cry Wolf,* happily a film dear to April,
to help the facts be known.
She needs little convincing, actually, that the wolf is a noble being
observing up close as she does its closest kin
in our noble-hearted German Shepherd.

October 1987

Until We Can

May they treat him with care until we can.
My son sleeps tonight in Hong Kong.
We can't yet dream over his picture,
but still we can dream.
Against king-sized young fears he waits helplessly.
Half a world away we too wait helplessly,
trusting against king-sized fears of our own
that they're treating him with the utmost of care
until we can.

October 1987

Pity Texts Restricted To Prose

Books on parenthood don't so much err as fall short.
Parenthood is a journey unparalleled,
awe translated into service,
a discovery of self as much as the child,
a launch pad truly to support a lift-off.
The presence of whatever one calls the underpinning of the
    universe
is experienced so purely in a child's presence,
in the astounding emergence of a new human personality,
that the vast majority of parents on Earth (I've taken a survey)
would trade it for nothing.
Pity texts on parenting restricted to prose
when the subject matter is sheer poetry.

October 1987

First Finn Family Howl

No sooner back from my walk with the dogs,
I was ambushed right there in the kitchen
by monster daughter in arms of monster wife.
In the middle of a giggling snuggle and hug,
April led the way in a hilarious howling
which felt rambunctiously right for the love we were feeling.
Blessings on this wolfish evening
of the first Finn family howl.

November 1987

Banana Pudding Gift From The Blue

Penny's instinct was right
to invite April to our banana pudding treat.
Long in bed she was still chirping happily
to herself or her encircling furry friends.
That it was so late and we had to get her up early tomorrow
prompted a quick no from me,
but then I got to thinking
it's not like this is a common occurrence.
Why not splurge at times with a gift from the blue,
for no good reason except that it feels right to have a party?
Good idea, let's do it, I heard myself agree,
and soon with eyes aglow and glee spreading wide April bounded
    joyously into the kitchen
for a banana pudding gift from the blue.
If ever I search for an image of grace,
I need only remember from this evening
April's ecstatic face.

November 1987

What's The Big Deal?

April pitched a fit today.
When she kept demanding dessert before its time,
I ushered her to her room for a time out.
Not liking it one bit,
she then began shrieking and stomping.
Lots of things run through your mind when your kid throws a
    tantrum,
like evaluating whether the issue at stake calls for resolute
    unbending
or whether just maybe fatigue and frustration contributed to
    overreaction on Daddy's part.
Even when satisfied you made the right move,
there are considerations about safety and time, strategies for
    reconciliation.
This time I did some minor compromising
by responding to her prolonged sobbing with a hug
which seemed to help break the downward spiral.
Soon we returned hand in hand to the kitchen
where, without fanfare, she finished her meal, as if what's the big
    deal?
After which Daddy lauded her with superlatives about such a big girl
    to turn it around,
clarified what we could learn from it,
and, last but not least, dished up dessert.
This one, I think, led to some growing—
just let me not wait for another tantrum
before dispensing with hugs and superlatives.

November 1987

Where You Have Silly

Our richest family times are when we're the silliest.
Spaghetti pile-up on the waterbed is huge fun
as is suspenseful hiding culminating in gleeful capture.
Our current giggling game is where one calls the others the silliest
    while claiming to be the sane and stable one
with the others stoutly protesting, of course, that it's just the
    opposite,
and then the roles change and the alliances change
with nothing making a lick of sense except the giggling.
I've come to believe where you have silly,
you're very likely not only to have love but to keep it.

November 1987

She's Beginning To Be Captured

April still likes the pictures but now sees the words.
"What does that say, Daddy?"
Ah, it's beginning.
Soon the attraction will be irresistible—
she'll not only want to know what more of them mean,
she'll want to start reading them herself,
then writing them!
Before fatherhood (in what feels like a former life)
I figured between first words and puberty—
with the exception maybe of starting school and riding a bike—
nothing much dramatic happened.
Chalk it up to ignorance.
She's beginning to be captured, my daughter of 3,
by the lure of living words!

November 1987

Soon Christmas Tree Hunting

Richness is approaching.
Soon I'll take April Christmas tree hunting,
let her help me pick one out,
say a prayer of thanksgiving to a generous being for its giveaway of
    life,
then bring it back home for a metamorphosis into shining.
Even those indifferent to Jesus' birth
must in some hidden recess stand spellbound
before the resplendence of the tree of life.
It's joyous to introduce the richness of it
to a girl herself resplendently shining.

November 1987

There's Nothing Easy About It

I just warned April she'd better not give me a hassle
when I wake her early tomorrow for preschool.
It's well past bedtime and she's in there still chirping.
It won't be sweet those first few minutes,
but I find it helps if I anticipate it with her,
remind her a whining "Leave me alone!" won't cut it,
that if she chooses to stay up tonight
then she'll take her knocks tomorrow without taking it out on the
  world—
otherwise end of late privilege.
A parent's job, as I see it, is to progressively allow more choice
on condition consequences are understood.
There's nothing easy about it,
either the teaching or the learning of responsibility.

December 1987

Poor Training For Life

A friend of mine who's a parent once told me his rationale for
    spanking—
how he employed it sparingly, only on serious matters, to make a
    dramatic point,
how it lingered in his kids' memory as a salutary reminder.
I heard just last week
this same friend say to his 3-year-old daughter,
"If you don't swallow that food, you're going to get a spanking."
Serious matter?
What does "sparingly" come to over the years
when convenience and efficiency conspire against it?
Let's face it, physical threat gets prompt attention, desired action.
But even if it is only used sparingly, with salutary memory
    lingering,
do we really want our children to obey
ultimately so they won't get whacked?
Military discipline, however requisite for war, is poor training for
    life.
For not swallowing food?

December 1987

A Kick In The Pants

I wasn't at my best today.
Some days you're just on—
you say the right things, make the right moves, feel in accord and in
    flow.
I have these days sometimes with April,
when present moment opens gracefully into the next present
    moment.
Today was not one of those days.
Today, with multiple clashes and testing and tears, had nothing
    graceful about it.
While I'd like to chalk it up to a 3-year-old doing her thing,
I know a major part of it was me.
Package wrapping and envelope sealing,
then hurried assault on more than normal dirt and clutter,
left little real time for April.
And I wonder why the clashes?
Even when I'm "on," there'll be confrontations of will, after all
    she's 3,
but today I lay it on me.
May this serve as a kick in the pants
to remind me of the predictable consequences
when I don't put first things first.

December 1987

Shrine Of Innocence

Looking down on a child's sleeping face,
wondrously your own child,
floods the heart with a tenderness beyond expressing,
makes the universe, at least for the moment, softer,
the Earth dearer,
life holier.
Awestruck before a shrine of innocence,
the pilgrim in a parent's heart can only bow.

January 1988

But Some Are Decidedly Brighter

Drawn to her room by the conversation,
I spied April lying on her back,
legs vertical against the top bunk's frame,
paging through the tiny New Testament given by a friend
while narrating the imagined contents in alternating stern and
    singsong
to attentive animals gathered around.
Talk about stream of consciousness.
Freud would have loved it had he comprehended its source.
I did all I could not to crack up,
then trailed off in fascination of her spirit, in love of her dearness.
How perfect that Penny joined in the listening,
making for the kind of communion that validates parenthood.
No moments are more God than others,
but some are decidedly brighter.

February 1988

Focusing On Just One Gift

A rich musing for any evening
is to focus one's total attention on just one gift received,
one gift of such stabbing beauty and meaning
that remembrance of it even in darkness
floods with enough breathtaking radiance
to justify the entire sweep of a life.
Just a father musing on a February evening
on how the single gift of his radiant daughter
justifies the entire sweep of his life.

February 1988

Savoring An Apparition

April just wobbled out of her bedroom.
Barely able to see through squinting grogginess,
in swift order she requested I turn on the humidifier (seems we
    forgot),
turn the light all the way up (you never know when you might want
    to read),
and fill her cup (which she promptly again emptied).
Then it was back to bed for a tender tuck-in and bunny-nuzzle.
I drift sweetly awhile in the ensuing stillness,
savoring an apparition.

February 1988

Charles C. Finn

A Singular Gift

Biological parents can't help but feel
just the slightest pity for adoptive ones.
The genetic bond is lacking, the blood connection,
the indescribable early bondings during and after birth.
Lacking this foundation, how can the grounding be as firm?
That's how I used to think.
Having thwarted the initial dream,
destiny then bestows on adoptive parents a singular gift:
the revelation that blood connection is not essential,
rather that beneath familial, ethnic and racial variations
the same blood flows through a single family.
Biological bonds are lacking only if you don't look deep enough,
and pity is only fitting if you fail to fathom
the indescribable bondings during and after adoption.
Parents about to adopt have awaiting them a revelation.

February 1988

First Gymnastics Class

Seeing her perky pride and sunburst glee
bouncing and tumbling every which way
twirling over bars with guiding
beaming even when unbalanced
stirred her father's heart, now softening, now swelling,
past telling.

March 1988

Best Friend

What stride towards personhood,
boost to self-esteem,
to have somebody to talk about at home who's also 3
and who's your best friend!

April 1988

Embodiment Of Wonder

Curious George is one of April's favorites—
the little monkey whose curiosity invites all manner of scrape
from which he not only manages somehow to escape
but in the process to become a hero.
I love explaining to her what curious means in terms of herself—
no fancy airs,
impish explorations,
questions artless and pure.
What philosophers proclaim an essential for wisdom,
what Jesus holds up as a prerequisite for the kingdom,
what Curious George exemplifies endearingly in his adventures,
I, gifted being called father, behold daily
in embodiment of wonder called daughter.

May 1988

Lollygagging With Style

"Daddy," she said pertly, coming from her room well past bedtime,
"I'm just going to have to get rid of this book—
it's a children's book but I like animal books."
Called delaying tactic by some,
ploy by others,
lollygagging by us,
it's often part of April's ritual of decline.
I decided to yield a little,
merely to look stern as she walked saucily to my study with book
    under arm and peek over shoulder,
assuring me she wouldn't go in the office but only put it inside the
    door.
You see, one of Daddy's rules is stay out of the study.
So cute was she in deferring to this injunction
while strutting her stuff in stretching another,
that it was hard to look stern.

May 1988

Dipsydoodlers

Listening to late night jazz calls to mind a game April and I play.
When we get near her preschool in the morning,
she cues me with "dipsydoodle"
at which point I swerve off course for a curlicue detour
with both of us exclaiming in feigned dismay,
"Oh dear, how will we ever find our way?"
In the nick of time, though, we do find our way back,
heave a huge sigh of relief,
and then have a good laugh at our silliness.
Jazz musicians might well be the original dipsydoodlers— seeming
    ever to swerve off course
but managing not only to find their way back but to have such a
    musical time of it
on their improvisational curlicue detours.

May 1988

Not Yet 4 But Soaring

"I want to be a teacher just like Annamarie."
When your child, not yet 4, already soars with aspiration,
it endears you to said teacher for demonstrating
that this thing called learning can be so filled with the fun of
  discovery
that her students (one of whom is your very own daughter)
start dreaming of passing it on.
Preschool sounds ho-hum until it's remembered
what can get ignited there.

June 1988

Aching Realization

On the excited brink of becoming 4,
April assured me during our bedtime ritual
that when 4 she can still be picked up by me
but that after 5 she'll be too big.
I said that's fine with me, girl.
Moments later she casually slipped it in
that I can pick her up even when she's 6
but that after that she'll be too big.
With a smile that forced an impish grin,
I said that's fine with me, girl,
aching to realize that whichever the year,
the time will come (as she aches to realize too)
when she *will* be too big.

June 1988

Ah, But Not So

A 4th birthday may sound no big deal,
just one of those nondescript years between toddlerhood and
    kindergarten,
ah, but not so.
Consciousness is dawning with such exquisite subtlety and occasional
    prodigious leap
within this vivacious whole human being
that to be on the actual brink of 4 (which means no longer 3!)
seems as unimaginably wonderful to her as it does to dumbfounded
    me.

June 1988

I'm Going To Marry Daddy

I told April today that when she grew up
she'd find somebody to marry and have children of her own.
Her soft but emphatic answer: "I'm not going to get married,"
adding seconds later, "I'm going to marry Daddy."
If they hadn't been all along,
I'd say things were getting interesting.

June 1988

When Children Regress

Parents have a difficult challenge when their children regress—
if too attached to steady progress, retreat will seem defeat
and disappointment (or worse) will get communicated.
What children least of all need
when insecurity and fear prompt retreat
is to feel the bite of their parents' blame—
first failure, then shame.
If ever unconditional love, mommy and daddy, now!

June 1988

Pretty Nifty Scheme Of Things

"Daddy, are you pulling my leg?"
April couldn't get over it when I told her water for our living—
without which the plump grapes of us would turn into juiceless
    raisins—
comes not really from faucets
but from underground reservoirs saving the rain!
It's a pretty nifty scheme of things
that for 42 years past her 4 I still can't get over.

June 1988

I'll Play Their Game

The adoption agency is concerned that I broke with Catholicism,
changed so drastically that I now attend Unity,
perhaps am too unstable to parent.
I suppose they have to be careful,
be on the lookout for danger,
but misperceiving spiritual evolution belies sad definition of
    danger.
But of course to get our son I'll play their game.
I'll not let on not even Unity is home,
realistically not expecting to find one
given the nature of creeds and dogmas and such.
Neither will I whisper this poem in their ears
lest from dangerous talk of spiritual evolution
they find suspicion of instability confirmed.

June 1988

Necessary Disillusionment Coming

One of the poignancies of parenthood is knowing what's coming.
Our daughter's need one day will be to become disillusioned with
    us,
painfully to discover and throw off our ambiguity and shadow
if some later day to have a good shot at becoming reconciled with
    her own.
May we find the pluck to keep loving, even the wisdom to bless,
when in disillusionment she rebels in order to move on.

June 1988

Fingers Still Thumbs

Patience doesn't come easy for a girl just turned 4
whose eyes are set in earnest on the goal of tying her shoelaces.
Some in preschool already can do it so the pressure's on,
but, alas, her fingers are still thumbs.
Again and again she tries,
each time with frustration though she's getting closer.
She doesn't want to ask for help—little kids do that—
but what a bind it leaves her in:
do for yourself what you can't yet do for yourself
and when you really can't you can't admit it.
Daddy has a delicate job here—
not to jump in too eagerly (hardly a vote of confidence)
but to be quick to congratulate the determination to try
and be ready with a suggestion to work as partners
before the frustration mounts too high.
Turning 4 has its challenges for both daughter and Daddy.

June 1988

On Independence

Two grand achievements of late—
tying her shoes all by herself
and, without any help, singing "America the Beautiful" to the end.
Ecstasies of 4 can be the purest
when independence, as vital as that declared by a nation at birth,
is not only declared but achieved!

July 1988

May She Not Be Stung

Three hornet nests this evening
bit the dust by way of conflagration,
their assembled ferocity no match for gasoline ignited.
Live and let live is a commendable philosophy,
but insects force some exceptions.
No disparagement intended to hornets, themselves playing a role in
    the whole,
but their attack against an accidental intrusion—
with near catastrophic consequences for a friend allergic—
brought their threat home last night.
In some spiritual circles this is betrayal of the Great Harmony
    vision,
of the mandate to universal stewardship,
but if three hornet nests aren't destroyed
my daughter scrambling in play has an excellent chance of scrambling
    the wrong way
and paying for it dearly.
May she not be stung by my spirituality.

July 1988

Putting It Squarely

"I don't want my baby brother to come.
I don't want to share mommy and daddy with him.
If he comes, you won't love me any more."
I couldn't believe she was putting it so squarely,
and she just turned 4.
I don't think my response did justice.
I reassured her of our continued loving
and how no one will ever replace her in our hearts,
which needed to be said.
But I wish I had congratulated her more for sharing these things,
empathized more with how scary it must feel,
emphasized more how natural these feelings are when a newcomer
    comes
and how good when they're expressed
because it gives mommy and daddy a chance to say just how much
    and for always they'll love her.
Hmm, not saying it then
doesn't mean I can't say it now.

July 1988

Girls' Night

It's girls' night for Penny and April—
a slumber party of two with the ambitious aim of movie-watching
    all night.
I'll likely be tucking them both in around 11:30,
but how joyous their glee in anticipation of such camaraderie.
Mine is a softer glee,
listening from my study to eruptions of laughter
from an ancient camaraderie.

July 1988

A Challenge To Match Any

"He needs a father at his age."
"Yeh, a father makes all the difference."
Back-to-back cliches from *The Natural*,
but cliches become so for touching truth.
Being the kind of father a child at any age needs
is a challenge to match any.
Can a vocation for a man be higher than fatherhood,
more rigorous, more rich?

July 1988

Reassuring Foreshadowing

What is each night's falling into the abyss of sleep
but a reassuring foreshadowing of the awesome final falling?
I've been gazing on April
drifting in a skiff of trust over an ocean called sleep.
It came time to yield and without the slightest fear she yielded.
It seizes my heart to see the perfection of her innocence frail against
    the night.
I fear her eventual bruising,
pray her full unfolding,
vow protection to her,
bow to God in her,
see in the magnitude of her surrender, of her trust in morning's
    calling,
a reassuring foreshadowing of how each of us can meet
that awesome final falling.

July 1988

Apparition Of Innocence

"I love you, Daughter of the Sun"—
then a kiss on the cheek and I'm gone.
When the 4-year-old light of my life
asks for water in the night and I take it to her,
my act of service brings instantaneous reward—
an apparition of innocence secure in love
surrendering again to sleep.
A kiss on the cheek and I'm gone.

August 1988

The Security Of Consistency

Accepting limits occurs only after losing battles.
We're having to lean on April these days,
impress on her who's boss,
establish for her if not understanding at least the security of
consistency
which ranks high on the list of needs of a 4-year-old bound and
determined to bow to no limit.
Taming and guiding, yes,
curbing spontaneity, after a fashion, yes,
breaking spirit, pray God never.

August 1988

To Get The Job Done

Even when parents make the time to talk frequently,
it's tough as hell to get the job done—
to be consistent,
back each other up,
not allow the child to divide,
carry discipline through at figurative gunpoint,
keep congratulating each other through the fray and sometimes
 dismay of it.
What must it be for a child
whose parents do *not* make the time to talk frequently?

August 1988

In Need Of A Little Sweetness

April suddenly hates kisses but allows an exception.
If late in the evening a butterfly happens to land softly on her cheek
around the time Daddy tucks her in,
well, you can't fault a butterfly in need of a little sweetness,
now, can you?

September 1988

Smurfy Fantasy

Spying me writing in the living room,
April called out from her bed that she's going to write poems too
    some day.
Then she can read mine and I can read hers.
Great idea, I responded, meaning it.
She had asked me just prior if my Daddy had taught me to write
    poems when I was a little boy.
I said no, my Daddy never went in for writing poems, not even
    reading them.
Children aren't like their Daddies in every way, I said, and that's
    okay.
I made it more specific.
And when you grow up, April, you'll probably want to do a lot of
    other things besides writing poetry,
and that's great.
That's when she assured me to the contrary.
How I love the Smurfy fantasy
of reading my poems to my daughter some day
and then listening to hers.

September 1988

Drawing The Line

April spent the better part of the morning confined to her room.
Let's just call it a long time-out.
We even stayed home from the library and gymnastics, and a
    restaurant in between,
due to her dug-in heels.
Flexibility is a parental prerogative, but sometimes a line has to be
    drawn.
She's got to learn she doesn't call the shots,
that if she bucks the system, the system will buck back harder.
She finally straightened her room and we had a fine rest of the day
(sans library, gymnastics, and restaurant in between).
I hope she got the point.

September 1988

A Thing For Animals

April's got this thing for animals—
she's fascinated with them,
somehow feels kin to them.
When playing with kittens at home she's in her element.
In our weekly outing to the library,
her criterion for rejecting a book is it's not about animals.
The trip to the pet shop is a treat every time,
and what adventure is each venture to the zoo.
Already she's learning from animals past any school's capacity to
   teach.
Some bright day when she discovers Native wisdom,
its reverence for every living thing and particular regard for animals
   as teachers,
from the soul of her she'll sing.

September 1988

Beneficiary Yet

One of the achings over my father's passing
is knowing my daughter will grow up untutored by the steadiness
    and humor,
the gentleness and honesty,
of her Granddaddy
except insofar as these his dearest gifts
come to be so imbedded in those he steadfastly loved, like her
    daddy,
that those he in turn steadfastly loves, like his daughter,
will be beneficiary yet of her Granddaddy's dearest gifts.

September 1988

Suddenly Not Such A Bad Idea

Realistically unsettled at the prospect of a brother coming
with poignant expressions of loss and fear,
April just learned with happy amazement that her good friend Jon-
    Michael,
when his own baby brother arrived,
himself received gifts!
A baby brother coming suddenly holds possibilities
not altogether unpleasant.

September 1988

Distinct Possibility

We may just have seen a picture of our son—
a boy in Hong Kong up for adoption
with special needs past what we had expected.
We need our doctor's input before summoning courage to decide,
but it's a distinct possibility that a boy of 13 months
staring at us in a snapshot from the other side of Earth
whose birthday coincides with my deceased sister's
just might turn out to be (good God) our son.

October 7, 1988

We Went And Did It, Girl

There comes a time, after pros and cons have had it out,
after analysis and intuition have been accorded their due,
when you leave off sorting out and sifting through
and let your heart shout.
We went and did it, girl—
that far-off little one, as of this evening's monumental decision,
of all the boys across the Earth
is to be our son!

October 10, 1988

Roots Or Wings—Either Way You Empower

It's a hard choice when naming a child—
do you honor a family member
and by extension an entire bloodline,
or do you honor a dream,
an intimation of a hope in line with your highest wish?
Continuity or creation,
roots or wings—
either way you empower
when you give your child a name!

October 1988

Son Of The Red Earth

It came out of the Monday blue.
In all our prior musing, neither of us had considered Adam
as a possible name for our son.
But today when Penny called, after learning it means "son of the red
　　Earth,"
we both knew instantly his name would be Adam.
He'll grow to be a man, this Adam of ours—symbolically the first,
born of our red Mother,
father of a race to come.
May he find fruit for his innocence and awakening
before taking leave of our garden.

October 17, 1988

Holy Undertaking

It's a holy undertaking to search for a name for a child.
April was young enough when she arrived
that we gave her a Korean middle name
holding more meaning for us than her original.
But our son will be 18 months before he arrives from Hong Kong
so to change the name he's used to
not only will make a hard transition harder
but somehow feels untrusting of destiny.
I'm beginning to see more clearly as Penny has from the start
that our son and destiny will be more honored
if we keep his Chinese middle name.
May Adam Yau Kam Finn
be a name he richly lives with.

October 1988

October Evening

At April's instigation we packed a picnic dinner and headed to the
    pond.
After Penny and April fished while I tended the fire,
there followed scrumptious eating after wiener and marshmallow
    roasting,
snuggling together in the sleeping bag,
and singing songs to the emerging stars.
A stunning crescent moon simply confirmed
we'd long remember the fun and beauty
of this crisp October evening

October 1988

Less Logic Than Leap

Logic carries only to the brink.
He's just past 1,
way underweight from premature delivery,
neck abnormality already treated,
facial birthmark making adoption unlikely in his country of birth.
After you try computing it rationally, there's nowhere to go but
　　your gut,
to your inner sanctuary's silence.
Do I dismiss as irrelevant that his birthday is the same as my sister
　　now gone?
Important life decisions
sometimes call less for logic than a leap.

October 1988

Journey Of Delight

A 400-mile car trip
with a 4-year-old for my sole companion
has more potential for ordeal than delight
which underscores the measure of my amazement
upon completing with said companion an 8-hour journey
of nearly uninterrupted delight.

October 1988

One Last Hug

"I love you so much I want to give you one last hug"—
nearly irresistible even when the ploy is transparent.
It'll buy her another minute maybe before finally having to call it a
    night.
Disinclined as girls of 4 are to head for bed, even when eye-rubbing
    tired,
we allow a little lollygagging until it's time to draw the line.
Thank goodness there was still time tonight
for one last hug.

October 1988

Amazing Already The Journeying

A friendly question to April from the hairdresser:
"I hear you're going to be a big sister."
The matter of fact response: "I already *am* a big sister.
I have a brother in Hong Kong."
Penny and I beamed.
But a few months back she was emphatically entrenched
against the very notion of a brother coming.
Amazing already the journeying
within the mind of a girl of 4.

October 1988

Disappearing Peas

The disappearing peas worked again tonight,
only this time it was Tylenol.
April's been running a fever, felt punky enough to go to bed early.
To help her rest easier, I went in to give her some Tylenol,
but she wanted none of it.
What she wanted was for me to leave her alone.
That's when I resorted to my old ploy.
Back when she just started eating solid foods,
we played this very fun game where Daddy lined 5 to 10 peas in
     front of her,
then turned his back pondering out loud,
"Surely none of those peas is going to disappear
when I count to ten and turn around."
How pleased she was every time
at my astonishment over the peas' disappearance.
Well, sick as she was tonight,
she just couldn't let those two Tylenol sit there
while, back turned, Daddy was counting to ten.
May she be resting easier.

October 1988

Lullaby And Heart-Song

The bedtime ritual keeps changing.
I'm to sing two songs now,
the lullaby I've sung since her infancy ("Like a Ship in the Harbor")
    and a "Heart Song."
That's when Daddy just starts adlibbing it softly—
it may start out with the heart of tree or mountain, sunflower or sun,
    Care Bears or Grandfather,
but it always manages to come back to our own hearts circling blood
    through us,
uniting us with the heart of the universe that circles atoms into
    dancing and stars into galaxies.
I must admit my fancy wheels free here,
but she keeps asking so it must be connecting.
Maybe it's the whimsy
or the wide-ranging reverence
or the silly-soothing ticket to wind-down and sleep.
Whichever it is I hope this one won't soon be changing.

October 1988

Till I'm About 10

"Put Dracula's teeth and cape away till I'm about 10.
I want to be a bunny rabbit."
It's nice that she can put off
what she knows she's not ready to face.
It pierces the heart to know some 4-year-olds
lack the power or say to keep dragons at bay.

October 1988

Partnership

Penny gave me feedback I resisted at first hearing.
I've been letting April slide—
telling her to do things but then letting her take her merry time
until I sound stern and she hops, less obedient than intimidated.
So we had a serious talk, April and I, that won from her less than a
ringing endorsement:
"That was a very LONG serious talk!"
It's only been two days but I can see a difference—
when I tell her to move, she moves.
She only tested me once and swiftly found herself in timeout.
The moral of the story:
you're lucky if you have a perceptive spouse willing to lay it on the
line,
trusting that your capacity and willingness to amend
outweighs your inclination to defend.

November 1988

Courtesy Doesn't Come Easy

Courtesy is hardly inborn if my daughter of 4 is any indication.
April's starting to ask with "please" and say "thank you" upon
    receiving
only after months of persistent shaping.
While we want her to honor her own wishes,
she needs to learn she's not the center of the universe
(except in a deeper sense she'll come to later)
which means others are to be accorded the respect of a thank you
    and a please—
not exactly a lesson she's learning with ease.

November 1988

To The Size Of A Home

The very word "Korea" lures me into a pleasing reverie.
It used to be for Penny and me but one Asian country among many,
of interest perhaps politically but never poetically,
until Life once upon a magical time bestowed on us
the breathtaking blessing of a Korean daughter.
Nothing succeeds like foreign adoption
in shrinking Earth to the size of a home.

November 1988

A Sacrificial Spirit

I was asked by a friend today, "What's the single most essential
    factor in being a good father?"
and heard myself answering, "a sacrificial spirit."
Parenthood and priesthood
have surprisingly much in common.

November 1988

Hungry In Their Soul

Instead of Science call it The Allurement of the Cosmos
or Enamorings of Matter and Reason.
Instead of Religion call it Consciousness Awakening to Union
or Spirit's Manifold Reaches.
Instead of Liberal Arts call it Visions Made Flesh
or Wild Achievements of the Human.
Call it what you will but teach it with love
because kids are hungrier in their souls than they or we know.

November 1988

Eyes Lighting Up Like Stars

4 is a very important age
and when the day magically arrives when now you're 4 and a *half,*
you can't conceal your glee just to think of it.
Tomorrow becomes deliciously anticipated
because then you can tell all your friends at preschool, "Guess how
    old *I* am!"
What privilege to be the father of a universe expanding,
eyes lighting up like stars to the wonder of herself.

December 1988

Banquet Feeding Soul

I took April tonight to the Harvest Moon banquet—
it was a nice chance to dress up,
eat delectable Korean cuisine,
catch up on other adoptive parents,
and marvel both at the gala gowns and how much the kids have
    grown (has it really been a year?).
Two pleasures this evening for my soul:
first, to fairly feel the world shimmer, somehow both shrink and
    expand,
just to see the roomful of us chatting,
embodying friendship across Earth
standing witness to Gaia's dream;
and then to see it in April's eyes, the light brighten as she basked
    in it,
comprehending more deeply the richness of her roots.

December 1988

You Never Know

We were chatting back and forth—
she from her bed and me from my study—
about what she might be in that faraway place called grownup.
I reeled off ten or so possibilities, elaborating a little on each,
concluding she could be just about anything she set her heart on.
"Even a unicorn?"
"Well, you never know."
"I want to be a unicorn."
Conclusion reached, she was ready for sleep.

December 1988

Seoul Stirrings

Ranging emotions stirred in me tonight
as I watched the opening Olympic ceremonies
from the land of my daughter's birth:
wonder before such precision and color pageantry,
thunder resonance with dragon drum,
joy glimpsing a people's soul ancient yet still vital,
pleasure seeing April of the proud eyes swelling to take it in,
a wistful reminder that for all she has gained there are things she
    has lost,
a cherishing for the diversely-jeweled planet we all can call home.

December 1988

It Is Good

Putting up a Christmas tree with a 4-year-old
works best when there's no hurry,
attachment to symmetry,
or fuss over ornaments dropped.
Little for sheer joy compares when an angel crowns the
    collaboration,
lights first catch breath,
and daughter and father stand back from their creation
beholding that it is good.

December 1988

Uh Oh

April informed me after our trip to the mall
that she only asked two things of Santa, wanting to lessen his load.
Uh oh, I thought, and began coaxing.
At first she wouldn't tell me 'cause it was their secret,
but finally she did and thankfully in time
for a surreptitious final shopping.
Next year we don't wait till two days before Christmas
to make our visit to Santa.

December 1988

Home Again, Home Again

"Daddy, why do little kids need to have their parents close?"
The question came out of the blue from April's bedroom.
"So they feel safe and always loved."
Silence.
"Do you understand?"
"Yes. To market, to market, to buy a fat pig,
home again, home again, jiggedy jig."
Her question,
my response,
her understanding,
and finally her whimsical ditty
just gave an uneventful January evening wings.

January 1989

Imponderables

A child's arrival is incredible whatever the route.
Breathless we wait our son, already 15 months old.
The odds against his finding a home in Virginia
when born in Hong Kong
are staggering.
Parents of foreign adoption
are awed to ponder such imponderables
as chance and providence and destiny.

January 1989

Infusion

China's legacy—
ancient,
opposites dancing,
wise with reverence,
harmonious with Earth,
suffused with enduring Tao—
soon will infuse a family far away
with the arrival beyond fathoming of a son.

January 1989

Take That, Mr. Sun

Waking in her car seat with the blinding sun in her face,
April flailed out with the worst she could summon:
"Pooey!"
Her expletives will doubtless become more graphic
but never more emphatic.
Take that, Mr. Sun!
How nice that she trusted he could take it
and keep on shining.

February 1989

Thanks To His Sprinkling

Alex Haley cast a gem:
"Grandparents sprinkle stardust over children."
I bless my stars to see it happening daily.
How taken with each other are April and Grandfather,
how they trade wonder for wisdom
with each reaping joy.
What faith in stardust she will carry through her life
thanks to his sprinkling.

February 1989

Imagine Her Mommy's

Today April rode her first horse.
Oh, there had been ponies before at carnivals,
slow motion elephants and camels before at fairs,
but for a girl all of four and a half
this was a thrill beyond.
She must really be growing up if she can ride a horse in a ring
just like Mommy did when *she* was a girl.
If you think *my* joy is great
catching today's ecstasy in the eyes of my daughter,
imagine her Mommy's!

February 12, 1989

145

Just A Father Musing

Longing came first,
then Imagination and Memory,
now Understanding.
All along Spirit's sparkling
and titanic impish Will.
Just a father musing
on his 4-year-old daughter.

February 1989

An Ancient Loving

"An itty bitty ditty
from a little fat kitty
who, o what a pity,
lives in the city."
We had great fun tonight blending our impishness—
father and daughter merriment of the richest kind
couched in the comfort of an ancient loving.

February 1989

Precious Arrival

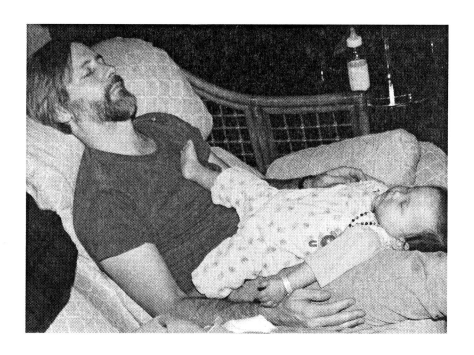

Double-zonked

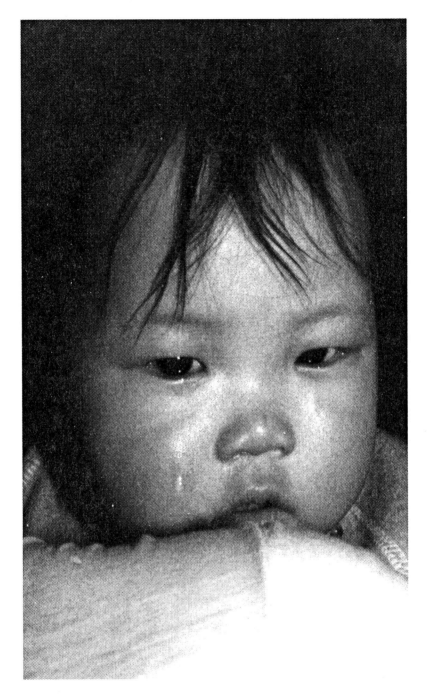

Some nights are long

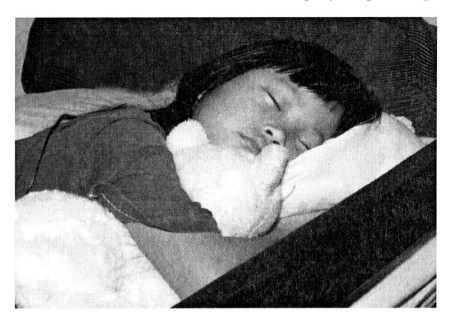

Innocence

Giggling and Grandfather

Big sister ambivalence

But we both love bunnies

Let me tell you, Mr. Santa

She can sleep with me

Little people need help sometimes

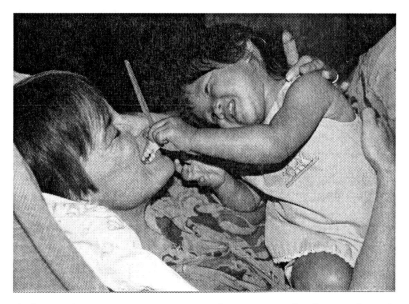

First Mommy gets *her* teeth brushed

Silly Granddaddy

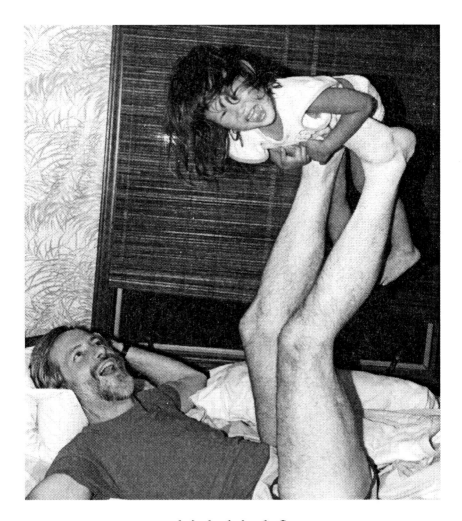

Whirlybird fun

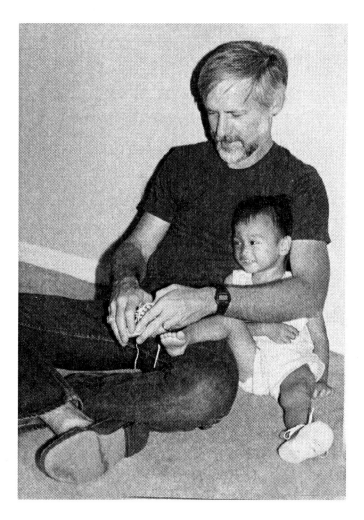

Trusting Daddy to help

Only the giggling makes sense

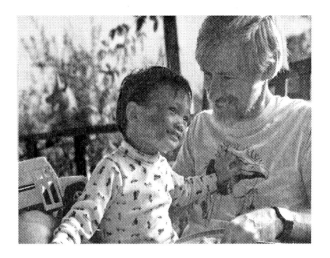

Joy in the moment

I can do it!

Grandfather flowing

Pride of first independence

I helped!

Roots

Witch and Pig

Princess

Let's get moving

Ample supply of reading material

First love

Kite-flying triumph

Accord

Comfort

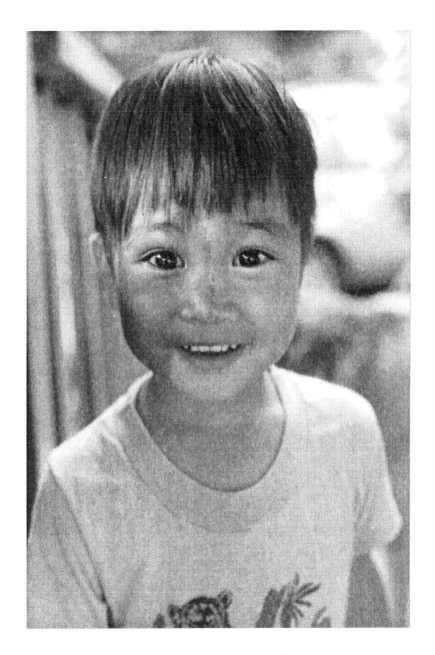

Here I am, world!

Son Joining

Imminent Ambush

Adam's arrival draws near.
It's an awesome event a new child coming
affecting an entire family a lifetime.
Destiny is ready to spring an ambush:
on us Adam's unique and living seed,
on him his mother's verve and versatility,
his father's steadiness and depth,
his sister's spontaneity and affection.
Fears of inadequacy diminish when, aeons in the making,
destiny's ambush is remembered.

February 1989

Month Dawns Diamond

Sometimes expectancy rides high as the sky,
like when a month dawns diamond
auguring the arrival of a child.
The son of our choosing
has found for many months insufficient wings to our arms
until March of 1989
which on the strand of other jeweled months
will stand out diamond.

March 1989

In The Guise Of Our Son

Our disbelieving in the literal existence of an historical Adam in
    Eden
wasn't in the least a deterrent in the naming of our son.
Mythic time transmuted by consciousness
becomes transparent of now.
Soon to arrive in the guise of our son
is not only the first man
but the father of a race to come.

March 1989

177

Ideals Instead Of Ancestry

The names we've chosen for our children
accent ideals instead of ancestry—
not easy on family members hoping for remembrance,
but then following inclinations of spirit
means loyalty sometimes to wider notions
of family and remembrance.

March 1989

She Knows The Score

She's struggling over his coming, and with good reason.
Try as we might to assure her of our love,
to appeal to her big sister status,
she manages lukewarm at best.
She knows the score.
She knows she's about to lose out in the shuffle—
it's tough seeing the big picture when you're all of 4.
It seems our most sensitive course
is to let her know it's okay to let out her sadness and fear.
Little kids, too, needs words for grieving.

March 1989

Steady, Heart

Steady, heart.
She said he'll be coming on the 31ˢᵗ if they can find that document.
At last we have a date to hang our hearts on,
heave our hope towards.
On the ultimate of this mountain of a month he will arrive
    transfiguring—
destiny-flung,
from China Sea's edge to valley in Virginia,
our son.

March 13, 1989

With Animals, Angels And Earth

Our final days of waiting for Adam
call to mind Joseph and Mary—
arriving in Bethlehem,
searching out shelter,
preparing swaddling clothes,
then with animals, angels and Earth
turning hearts inward to wait.

March 1989

Charles C. Finn

Countdown

In 96 hours
in a moment breathless
I'll behold and then hold
for the first time my son.
Natural delivery can't be quite so predictable,
but when you're talking foreign adoption
and know the exact hour when the plane will touch down,
you count down with confidence
(not to mention trepidation).

March 27, 1989

The Trip Of His Life

A little boy's in for the trip of his life to a far distant reach of Earth
where at first he'll fathom nothing and no one,
find his surroundings unfamiliar,
see faces unknown,
hear words unintelligible,
miss terribly everything that gave him security,
all who gave him comfort.
Hopefully after initial upheaval and stress
he'll come to discover reasons to bless
the trip of his life.

March 29, 1989

Lucky For Adam

During one of Adam's crying spells at the motel,
April so thrashed about in bed I assumed she was having a bad
    dream.
Today she identified the source of the thrashing,
but it was no dream.
"I was so mad at Adam last night
I wanted to put him outside and leave him there."
Let's just say that his big sister wasn't in charge
was lucky for Adam

April 1989

Difficult Nights

These are the difficult nights.
Around 11 he startles awake,
screams, it seems, as much from rage as fear.
Where's what I'm used to?
Who are these people and why don't they understand?
What has happened to my life?
Nothing soothes except being carried,
but the back can take but so much.
So we lie there in uneasy but essential presence
until exhaustion yields fitful sleep.
For two hours maybe
until he startles awake screaming and it begins anew.
Difficult nights.

early April 1989

Rough Early Going

"Mommy, I was so excited when Adam was coming I tap danced at
     the airport,
but I'm not so excited now and don't feel like dancing."
Perfectly put, little one.
None of us is much up for dancing just now,
but in time we will again (and with Adam joining),
in time we will again.

April 1989

Tightrope

She makes no bones about it.
"I hate him, I feel like kicking him."
Mind you, this was after a pretty good day—no overt squabbles,
she even fed him lunch and then had to call Mommy
in a flush of big sister pride.
It's not anything he's doing, it's that he *is*.
Call it bafflement over disentitlement,
rage over usurpation,
or grief over loss,
she's got more of each than she either comprehends or knows what
    to do with.
So we walk the tightrope—
while empathizing with her verbal and symbolic expressions of the
    most natural feelings in the world,
all the time reassuring with our love,
we make it clear as a bell that no matter how she feels
she's not to kick her brother!

April 1989

Far More Delight Than Travail

It's tempting to gloss over the travails surrounding our adopted son's
    arrival
given the chance he'll read it some day and perhaps reach the wrong
    conclusion,
but two reasons conspire to persuade me not to.
Other adoptive parents might be heartened to be reminded they're
    not alone,
and if my son *does* some day read these poems of his arrival,
I trust he'll not fail to find far more delight than travail.

April 1989

Early Confirmation

Hearing Adam imitate April's sounds,
from cat meow to squirrel screech to wolf howl,
and then their gleeful squeal after each,
was an early confirmation,
after a trying first week of transition,
that this family is going to make it.

April 1989

Nocturnal Relabeling

Relabeling makes a difference.
With a small child in the house again prospects are an eyelash from
    certain
that sleep for months will be drastically disturbed.
Dreading it in advance
leads to a cringe at the least stirring,
a mild curse (or worse) when the crying begins.
Expecting it, on the other hand, as a monk his bell to rise and pray
lends likelihood that thoughts of service
will soften the impulse to curse.

April 1989

Birthright Fire

Adam's refusal is dramatic.

He may not yet speak,

but his shake of head and scowl of face are unmistakable in
meaning,

and for the slow of learning he'll unleash in a flash the definitive
scream.

May we endeavor to temper but never extinguish his beautiful
birthright fire,

a volcanic legacy from the Earth

in need some day of his defiance for her healing.

April 1989

It May Well Take Years

It's ironic but hardly surprising that child number one
partially for whose sake we opted for child number two
is the one most unsettled by his coming.
Life was so rich with April
we were tempted to let that be it for our family,
but then we got to thinking what having a brother would teach her
    about give and take,
bring her in a sibling bond over a lifetime.
We haven't changed our tune
but realize now it may take years
for her to join in the singing.

April 1989

Where It Might Begin

If spanking is ever called for,
it's critical it not be administered under the influence of a drug or
 in anger,
otherwise God help small human being in the hands of one much
 larger
under the sway of an impulse to hurt.
Equating spanking with child abuse over-simplifies judgmentally,
but any decrying the inhumanity of the latter
hopefully will reflect soberly on where it might begin.

April 1989

Pearl Of A Seed

I was telling my daughter this evening,
in our thank you prayer for the day,
that the most valuable gift we can give to another is trust.
She's not likely to grasp it at 4,
so let's call it planting in a new garden
the priceless pearl of a seed.

April 1989

Spiritline

Nothing seems stronger than bloodline, ancestry cherished and
    perpetuated,
until you adopt.
Then is revealed the deeper secret, a richer legacy—spiritline,
a legacy bequeathed not through semen but through fertilizing song
    and vision.
Genealogists lament biological infertility
only by forgetting how spirit is born.
My children, remembering my song,
will inherit not my genes but my vision.

April 1989

Caught In A Crossfire

She's caught in a crossfire.
No longer content to be a mere 4,
April announces proudly she's 4 and 3/4ths,
inclines with her every fiber towards the Mecca of 5.
That is, most of the time.
Under sway of other realizations,
prompted in large measure by her baby brother's coming,
she plaintively wishes she were a baby again.
May our response spring from understanding.
May we trust she knows what she needs, even when it's regression.
May our arms ever be ready to enfold our baby.

April 1989

She Made It With Magic

Moving outward in space and backward in time,
our goodnight prayer covered plenty of ground.
When I arrived at the Big Bang birth of it all,
April's logical question was who made the Big Bang?
Deciding she's young yet for speculative flight,
I settled for the shorthand answer. "God."
"She made it with magic."
What could I do (smiling from my soul) but agree?

April 1989

The Source Now Of His Soothing

Still once or twice a night he screams awake,
then thankfully slips again to sleep with soothing.
Commensurate with our aching for the trauma of his transplanting
is our exceeding great comfort at being the source now of his
soothing.

late April 1989

Endearments

"I like you, Daddy.
Sometimes when I say I don't like you, I don't mean it. I'm just frustrated."

"That makes me feel warm all over, April.
We all say things we don't mean sometimes when we're frustrated.
Next time you say that to me, how would you like me to respond?"

"Just be quiet if I say that to you. Just let me say things.
I like you even though I say I don't like you. I still love you."

"And do you know even when I'm frustrated that I always love you?"

"Yes."

"Good night, April."

"Good night, Daddy."

May 1989

Dolphin Daughter

April took to the Medicine Cards right away.
They're about animals so they have to be good.
I have an intuition (along, I can't deny it, with a hope)
that the more she's exposed to Native spirituality
the more she'll frolic in its nourishing water
like a homecoming dolphin daughter.

May 1989

Parenting And Gardening Are Kin

Parenting and gardening are kin—
cultivating fertile ground for the sake of a miracle seed,
playing midwife to emergence fragile and slow,
bending back and knees so living things can grow.

June 1989

Secret Sorrow

April and I are hugely amused at the prospect of falling in a heap
    together
when I try to pick her up in the morning.
I've lamented that on her fifth birthday she may have become too big
    for carrying,
so she's been giving me impish directions on just how I'm to
    collapse.
"I'm so excited my toes are wiggling," she bubbled as I tucked her
    in.
Daddy's toes are quiet but his heart is not, comprehending with
    secret sorrow
she'll no longer be 4 tomorrow.

June 1989

Castle In The Air

Seeing April and Adam scramble, eyes bright with glee, in and out
    of their new tree house
filled their father's heart to brimming.
Honoring my instinct I videotaped it,
trusting it will be a cherished treasure for children grown some
    day.
A tree house all their own
with windows wide and wrap-around porch—
there's magic here!
In Joe we have a friend who knows how to make a thing,
a wizard waving wand called hammer until there it stands—
sure footing high up in persimmon arms,
a castle in the air!

July 1989

Budding Climber

Yesterday April asked Penny, "What are bellybuttons for?"
and ended up, after persistent questioning, learning ahead of schedule
    about the birds and the bees.
Today she asked me, "What are chanting monks?"
and ended up not only learning of AUM and Kyrie Eleison
but chanting them off and on through the day.
If sexuality and spirituality are mountain peaks of human essence
    and aspiration,
I'd say we have a budding climber.

July 1989

Eventful Venture

Two kids in a little red wagon
lugged perseveringly by steady daddy in the heat of a late summertime
    morning
found ample adventure.
The first delight were blackberries along the way—
ripe ahead of expectation,
not quite sweet as the raspberries,
inauspicious for erstwhile clean clothes.
Then it was the puddles from yesterday's rain—
thrilling especially to April with ankles all the way under, fanny as
    she crouched fairly touching.
Shortly thereafter a snake was spied, eyelevel on branch close to
    road,
quietly exchanging with us looks of suspicion.
While April and I confidently agreed it was a friendly one,
we gave it respectful wide berth and moved on.
As if our hour's entertainment with berries, puddles and snake
    weren't enough,
Periwinkle proudly then brought us a just won rabbit trophy limp in
    his teeth,
the kids marveling at its dead eyes unseeing.
Taking a cue from growling stomachs, we headed back for lunch,
April informing me along the way she was going to be a scientist
to see how bodies are made.
You never know when you venture out
what you'll venture on,
whose path you'll cross,
what awareness might dawn.

July 1989

No Other Way Worked

I get most impatient (angry if I'm honest)
when he sees me coming—even when I'm bringing what he's
    demanding—and still keeps screaming.
I literally have to quell an urge to out-yell him, an instinct to
    punish.
It helps remembering his stored-up pain,
how no other way worked to be noticed a year and a half in a crowded
    orphanage.
Against the instinct to punish
which would only confirm and deepen his desperation,
may I find patience born of understanding
to extend to his starving arms the comfort
he hasn't despaired, thank God, of still hungering.

July 1989

If Only I Can Swing It

Parenthood sometimes sucks.
My kid is shrieking at me for not paying him more attention,
for not doing as commanded.
I don't like to be screamed at
(hmm, perhaps in direct proportion to feeling guilty
for *not* paying more attention).
I cringe to see what it brings out in me.
Did I have to squeeze that hard?
Sorry, Adam, this is not a good day for me.
We need to sing a song or pounce on the waterbed.
I have no doubt you'll join right in
if only I can swing it.

July 1989

Encouragement Without Pressure

Two messages to April tonight at the pool:
"You can do it" while she peered over the edge of the diving board
weighing the wisdom of her first jump,
and "You'll know when you're ready and then you'll do it"
after she reached the speedy conclusion
that tonight was not the right night for a leap.
It's tricky communicating to your child encouragement without
    pressure

July 1989

Strong Winds

Penny describing Adam over the phone:
"His wide-open eyes take in everything.
When he's happy he throws his head back and laughs from his
    toes,
but does he have a hot temper—
when things don't go his way, he rears back and shrieks."
Wonder, laughter, fire:
strong winds to have at one's back embarking on life's bracing
    journey.

July 1989

Ambivalence Honored

"Are you excited about starting kindergarten?"
Despite the mistake of my leading question, April honored her
    ambivalence:
"I'm scared *and* I'm excited."
That she can own in her heart both shadow and sun
and be unafraid to give each expression
will serve my daughter well.

August 1989

Ah, To See The Bond Growing

I was struggling to figure out Adam's demand
when April, overhearing, said he wants his bottle,
and so he did.
"You see, Daddy," went her casual explanation,
"Koreans and Chinese understand each other."
Ah, to see the bond growing between sister and brother.

August 1989

I Can Do Better

I shook Adam harder today than I like writing about.
I've isolated it to the fact that I don't like being screamed at.
If I've been doing all I could, I resent his ingratitude.
If I've been non-attentive, I resent his truth.
Way too much resentment from one 47
to another not yet 2.
Sorry kid, I can do better.
I've got to do better.

August 1989

Loss Accompanying Gain

Granted she's been in preschool three years,
still entering kindergarten is symbolically big—for us as well
    as her.
Our daughter starts school tomorrow,
will go off in a big yellow school bus
leaving us in a cloud of dust and longing for simpler days and smaller
    world
with us securely at the center.
Gains to come are unmistakable,
ah, but for parenting cherishing hearts
each, in the way of things, will also bring loss.

September 1989

Go!

Whatever moves arrests him,
stirs some yearning, buried but burning, to hightail it out of here.
His favorite exclamation, most repetitious plea, (beyond even
    "mommy," "eat" or "no") is "go!"—
little difference if red wagon, stroller or car
as long as it moves and he's in it.
His fascination with the mechanics of things coupled with his love
    of motion
could end him up a racecar driver if he takes the notion.
Wherever he ends, towards whatever destination he tends,
inclined to curiosity and velocity he'll cover ample ground in getting
    there.
Bon voyage, son destined to travel, already come a long way,
may as you go you see beauty, spread kindness, learn the joy all
    Earth sings.
May wheels become for you wings!

September 1989

I Just Might

"Daddy, are you going to write your poetry tonight?"
"Yes, April, I think I will."
"Will you write about me?" she breaks into a smile.
Returning the smile, "I just might."
"Write about me and my bunny."
"Well, I don't usually know ahead of time what wants to be
    written,
but I just might."
That was an hour ago
and now as I gaze upon beauty that stabs me—
daughter asleep with arm around bunny—
I understand the perfection of her request
and can only try.

September 1989

Converging Inheritances

To the degree you cheer your ancestry, cherish your roots,
you mourn not passing them on.
There's grieving to be negotiated, make no mistake,
when biological offspring can't be.
But grieving softens as the realizations sink in
not only that my adoptive children will still inherit spirit legacies
     from my ancestral Ireland and Germany
but will commingle these with legacies coursing through their
     veins
from no treasure-realms less than Korea and China—
what converging inheritances to enrich!

September 1989

Joy's Pure Crash

When I asked April why such love for cymbals,
gleeful she swung windmill arms into colliding palms
exclaiming "because they go like that!"
Thanks to her perfect demonstration,
from now on when cymbals clash
I'll hear joy's pure crash.

September 1989

Charles C. Finn

Each A Mighty Confluence

April and Adam's inheritance
will fuse genetic gifts from distant Earth reaches
with heart and soul gifts from Penny and me.
Do we not all stand strong and stand tall
(if only inner eye sees)
to find ourselves at the mighty confluence
of proud ancient blood and bright new spirit?

September 1989

Mason Parents

Adam at age 2
still is in the forest primeval
from which instead of conscious memories he'll carry lasting
    impressions—
whether or not he is lovable,
his family is comforting,
the universe is trustworthy.
Day by day mason parents lay lasting foundation.

October 1989

Charles C. Finn

Glowing In A Glory

"What a great wind!" exclaimed April tonight, scrunching up her
    face in rapture.
Hey, that was my kid having a peak experience,
finding 5-year-old wings, suddenly soaring on them!
Hmm, is mystically-inclined daddy just projecting it,
reading his heart's hope into a mere expression of glee?
I laugh at myself for questioning what was transparent.
My daughter and I glowed in a glory tonight—
we cheered the big wind!

October 1989

Thank God For Suppositories

Having gotten food poisoning yesterday, Adam's having another
    night of it.
What's doing the trick—
stopping the vomiting and easing him to sleep—
is this little plug up his rear.
Usually it's Tylenol to this worried father's rescue,
tonight let's hear it for Phenergan.

October 1989

Some Are Driven

I find it necessary but insufficient
to lay upon myself the prohibition not to spank.
When a parent's ego has the upper hand and a child of two defies
    with screaming,
hands will squeeze enough to hurt,
voice will rise enough to frighten.
Easier said than done when by stress undone
to shift to a center deeper.
Some are lured to prayer by soft desire,
some are driven.

October 1989

Rescued From Snobbery

Youthful saleslady's response to my query about dragons:
"What's the difference between dinosaurs and dragons?"
Incredulous I could only mutter, "Dragons breathe fire and have
    wings."
Was she putting me on?
Could anyone culturally literate mix the two?
Ah, rescuing me from my snobbery came the understanding:
she must have no small children to keep her abreast of important
    things.
Smiling I resumed my quest for the magical serpent endowed of all
    things with fire and wings!

October 1989

Reality-Testing 101

As this is Reality-Testing 101 for April,
we figure we'd better give her some pretty accurate feedback.
When she's the quintessentially cute and dear 5-year-old, as I might
    add is most often the case,
we amply let her know so,
but so too when she's being a pain.
In our wind-down whimsy time tonight
I teased her a little about her not having been of the, let us say,
    sweetest disposition this evening,
to which she scrunched her face up in a mischievous grin
as if to acknowledge that our reprimand, earlier resisted when
    heard,
was not altogether unreasonable (and possibly even deserved).

October 1989

I Don't Care How Many Times

When your kid gets sick--
the fever kind with the obvious pain--
I don't care how many times it's happened before
still the fear gets to you.
It's getting to me right now.
Intermittently I go in with water or a cool cloth.
Then he'll drift off for a while,
and I hope the medicine's at last taking effect and that'll be it for the
    night.
But soon he cries awake with the fever he can't shake
making it a very long night.
I don't care how many times, it still gets to you.

October 1989

Tribute To A Medicine Man

To have young children not only like but trust their doctor
is a tribute not only to the skills but to the humanity of said doctor
who plies his artful trade, sacred profession
with sensitive word,
gentle touch,
eyes of compassion.
A good doctor is worth more than gold.

October 1989

She's Known It All Along

"I think Earth is father too"—
April's response to my prayertime praise of Earthmother.
Hey, my kid intuits androgyny.
Wait till she reads in Jung some day
about the animus within each female
comparable to the anima within each male.
She'll think she's discovering what she's merely recovering—
she's known it all along.

October 1989

Home At Last

It's taken him seven months
but finally Adam sleeps through the night.
No more startling awake, raging until held and soothed.
A wearying, worrisome seven months
o but the joy of a tender boy
secure enough at last, trusting enough at last,
to fall (and stay) asleep.
It's enough to make a father's soul thankful,
a father's heart sing.

November 1989

As A Matter Of Fact No

April asked me if I get lonely out on my late night walks.
I told her as a matter of fact no for I'm never alone.
Two dogs and a cat are with me,
the moon is sometimes with me,
planets and stars are with me,
presences of trees are with me,
pond and lookout point are with me,
unborn poems are with me,
God is with me.
I'm not saying she understood,
but she listened.

November 1989

Foe Into Follower

At first they'd do their separate things
with Adam unable to tag along for April's effort to ignore,
but now sometimes they play chase together,
build brick towers together serving as garages for their fleet
before tumultuous brick-tumblings to their feet.
After rage and confusion from little brother's intrusion,
it's affirmative of the resiliency of life to see a big sister regain her
    self-esteem and charge ahead again full steam,
discovering in the process that presumed mortal foe
lo and behold is now proud follower.

November 1989

A Contented Magical Spell

On our moonlit trek to Mt. Lookout,
thirteen horses grazing nearby came to check us out.
What a contented magical spell
with April in my arms nuzzling each in turn
amidst their standing curious prideful presence.

November 1989

Starting With Santa

My previous conviction about the healthiness of cultivating children's
    belief in magic
is confirmed now that I have my own.
April knows that most of the gifts coming will be from her family
    and friends,
but she also believes there's this man way up north—
jocund rotund good St. Nick,
friend of elves and reindeer and children—
who will somehow make it down the chimney
and leave when she's sleeping the gifts she asked for
and then pause to replenish himself for his journey with her thoughtful
    milk and cookies
before disappearing soft as a tinkling sleigh bell into the magical
    infinite night.
Of course there'll come a disillusioning when she learns Santa's not
    a literal fact,
but this can open rather than cripple her spirit if she begins to learn
    the great truth
taught gently by parents trying to live it
that no literal fact can contain the Mystery
which, behind metaphors starting with Santa,
keeps coaxing us towards it.

November 1989

Ripe For Crossing A Threshold

Last year April didn't dream of questioning it,
but this year she wonders if Santa really comes down that chimney.
She's still going along with things but getting ripe for crossing a
    threshold.
Her questions will find an honest response.
She'll need to hear when she's ready to hear
that yes Santa is real in that he's the spirit of giving,
the symbol of the great heart of humanity.
Whenever parents dispense gifts like Santa,
intangible ones even more than those wrapped,
they *are* Santa,
literally the great mythic man from the North
who flies guided by animal powers with gifts for the children of the
    world.
Were there a single historical Santa the magic would actually
    lessen.
April will hear all this, of course, in small doses,
but at five and a half she's already expanding
to the brink of beginning to glimpse the magnitude
of the meaning behind a marvelous myth.

December 1989

Santa Spending Himself

I observe Penny at Christmas spending herself—shopping, wrapping,
 mailing,
making stockings and costumes and cookies,
writing April a congratulatory letter from Santa for recent
 unselfishness with Adam,
finding hours to paint on April's first suitcase a rainbow over a
 unicorn in a field of flowers.
What do I see when observing her?
Santa spending himself, of course,
as children around the world,
with hope in their hearts and magic in their eyes,
thankfully can count on.

December 1989

Where Unicorns Roam

One of the advantages of being adopted
is you have two birthdays a year—
or more precisely in addition to a birthday a homecoming day,
an arrival day etched in an everlasting memory for the parents
to match any delivery room.
As for the child, it's a nice chance not only to have another party,
    with cake and even present,
but to re-listen, with each year's wider understanding,
to the wonder of a long ago turn of destiny
that against all odds on the wings of an angel
brought you to a magical kingdom where unicorns roam
called home.

January 1990

Controlled Spanking Test

As there's a controlled drinking test
to see if a limit can be set and stuck to with abstinence agreed on if
     unable,
so let there be a controlled spanking test
for parents judging it sometimes warranted.
Let them decide ahead of time, before frustration or fatigue clouds
     reason,
what imaginative alternatives they will try before resorting to
     physical force.
Let them also decide on a limit to the swats, as to how many and
     how hard.
The task then, like with alcohol, is to stick to the limit
or, that failing, to agree to abstain.
Children bruised into submission
either burn with memories a lifetime
or bury them so well they pass on the tradition,
which, from the standpoint of generations to come,
is worse.

January 1990

Way To Go, Little Unicorn

Not that I want him to stay there forever,
but a little longer would have been nice.
This morning when his car fell through the rungs, Adam figured
    why call Daddy
when all by himself he could climb down and get it.
Way to go, little unicorn,
sensing powers rising and fears falling and hearing open spaces
    calling,
you're no longer content with crib confinement.
Still, as a sigh escapes from a protective Daddy;
a little while longer would have been nice.

January 1990

A Joyous Aching

A small face pressed against the school bus window
brightens into a beam to see me waving,
a small hand waving back
rewards her father's being.
Both face and hand disappearing
in a fading roar around the bend
leave her father with a joyous aching
that somehow even when she returns doesn't end.

January 1990

To Remember And Build On

First of all we dealt with business—
clarifying how everybody's to pitch in to get done what needs
  doing,
then thrilling April with her first allowance!
Next we told each other what we appreciate but hadn't yet put into
  words.
Plenty of warm fuzzies to go around.
Finally came the chance to say what's bugging us and to request
  desired change.
No heavy deal, just a place for frustration to bear fruit.
It felt significant this first family meeting
which hopefully we'll remember and build on.
The Earth family, too, this very day has something to remember and
  build on:
Nelson Mandela walked free!

February 11, 1990

Magically Night Undone

No holier day's start
in predawn stillness
than arm around small son
while together watching Venus
draw forth with perfection
her most delicate rose.
Silent we took it in—
bright star,
snug and warm,
safe and dark,
Adam and Daddy.
Time out of time,
magically night undone,
father and son.

February 1990

He's Just Adam

I'm heartened to hear that the preschool kids
are as oblivious of his birthmark as are we.
Oh they noticed it and asked about it,
but then that's that and he's just Adam.
His big eyes and that grin,
his clutching hand and that emphasis
makes you only see endearing boy of not yet 3.
We all remember kids can be cruel,
but curious yet accepting seems the early rule,
and we're heartened.

February 1990

Daily The Lessons

My daughter confessed to me today
that she taught Adam once, or maybe it was twice,
to stick out his tongue at us,
but she thought he may have forgotten it
and she won't do it again.
I had been talking to her
about how the Finns and Millers believed in honesty,
and I guess to show she belonged
on a matter hitherto hidden she got honest
(not to mention the tenderest hug from her daddy
seized by her innocence).
Daily the lessons for her parents
from God age 5.

February 1990

This Girl's Heart Is Right

"Remember when you meet strangers, Mommy,
strangers need love too"—
a snatch from April I overheard the other day.
What compassion from a girl of 5
to counterbalance required caution.
Ah, at times it will cost her in tears,
but this girl's heart is right,
and mine cheers.

February 1990

C'est La Vie, Papa

"Some things are just not what you want, Daddy,
that's what life is all about."
It was her singsong tone of nonchalance
that got me as much as her words.
I forget the frustration of the moment,
but I'll always smile to remember and relate
how my philosophic imp of 5
tried to set me straight.

February 1990

Both Of Us Know

"When I grow up I'm going to be a teacher and a flyer and a
    mother."
She's been saying it now for months,
calmly, like she knows.
Now it may or may not be in a classroom,
but from what many have already learned,
I'll vouch she's got it in her to teach.
And she may or may not get a pilot's license, literally soaring up
    there,
but the burgeoning spirit of this pearl of a girl
unquestionably some day will soar.
And whether or not the biological kind,
there's no way this nurturing daughter of Gaia
will end up other than mother.
Both of us know.

February 1990

High Noon At Tombstone

Adam eagerly anticipates our library trips
for the little train in Lost And Found that he loves to pull around.
Well, today it was high noon at Tombstone,
for we arrived only to discover that another 2-year-old had
    commandeered the train!
All Adam could do was to glare at the thief
and shout "No!" each time she'd even look at a book that April or I
    would bring him.
I tried, of course, to reassure him that the books were his and safe,
but if somebody despicable can seize your train,
is anything safe?

March 1990

Diamond Moment

In darkness rocker,
in rocker mother,
on mother's lap daughter,
on daughter's lap brother,
from daughter soft lullaby
to brother nearing sleep,
for father overhearing
diamond moment to keep.

March 1990

Never Childish

There's all the difference in the world to a child's ears between
    shouldn't be afraid and needn't.
Shouldn't shames—
what's the matter with you, kid,
don't be so weak,
don't be such a baby.
Needn't coupled with explanation dispels darkness,
comforts with acceptance and reassurance,
doesn't demean.
Parents can't be too careful with their response
to a child's never childish fears.

March 1990

On Calming Fears

Allowing children their fears without chiding them for being
   childish,
comforting them with reassurance,
letting them know we've been scared too lots of times but it's all
   right now because we're near—
what more foundational way in the dragon lair of their early years
can we love our children, can we calm their fears?

March 1990

A Year To The Day

It's a year to the day since he descended from the blue.
This boy of 2 is a pistol.
Back and forth between energetic and at ease,
he's interested in just about everything—
especially if it moves!
But while action and motion are in,
hold please the loud bangs and roars.
Such a human little boy is our Adam
with inquiring eyes, strong demands, wide tendernesses.
Happy first year here, kiddo,
may you feel at last home.

March 1990

Courting The Big Wind

We had three kites up there today,
tails flirting, every which way wind-skirting.
Then to see vultures, gliding majestically, sail into view courting
 the big wind!
"Keep pulling, April, a little gust will catch yours back up there.
Now let it out slowly and start running, girl, and watch Pegasus rise
 and swirl!

April 1990

Hate Is A Potent Word

It's hard to know how to respond
when in a fit of anger April says she hates me.
I need to not overreact.
I need to keep remembering normal,
encouraging, in fact, that she can give her mad such clear and bold
    expression
and trust she won't be shamed or clobbered.
But hate is a potent word,
and she needs some caution about throwing it around,
some explaining how hurtful it can be.
Or do I ignore the word itself
and just let her know I hear the mad underneath
and am ready when she is to talk reasonably?
Sometimes it's hard to know.

April 1990

Crowded But Comfy

Adam's content for now to stay in his crib.
After discovering how to exit if he needs to, he chooses not to.
His bunk's all ready under April's,
but haven's comfort has yet to yield to adventure's lure
even though new truck, old teddy and longer legs
leave barely enough room for Adam.

April 1990

Back From The Toy Store Beaming

Back from the toy store beaming,
April informed me she was very wise—
instead of spending all her money for a big something,
she got herself a few special little somethings
and put the rest back into her savings.
How could I not agree
on the thorny subject of managing money
that this girl of deliberating heart and gleaming eyes
indeed was wise?

April 1990

Swept Up Sweetly

Dancing with my kids
ages five and two
first to the *Alleluia Chorus*
then to "I Heard It on the Grapevine"
provided us moments of purest joy
that hopefully this pen (inclined also to dance)
will help me remember.
Ah, to be swept up sweetly
with willing children and pen
into the Universe's dance!

May 1990

Just Like It Oughter

"And if you take my hand, my son,
all will be well when the day is done"—
at this point in our nightly song
Adam's and my hands find each other softly.
Then with April I add the verse,
"and if you take my hand, my daughter,
all will be well just like it oughter"
which usually gives us a good giggle.
Many are the tender moments
when nurturing the fragile magnitude of a child.
It's easier to accent parenthood's hassles and headaches
than its heart liftings, soul soothings, spirit absolute soarings.
All evolution rises up, the entire universe bows down
before the fragile magnitude of a child.

May 1990

From My Lookout On The Shore

Three times April's called to ask how we're doing,
    to tell us she's having fun.
I'd say she's missing us
just about exactly as much as we're missing her.
These overnights at friends mark the beginning of her
    venturing out over waters
I from my lookout on the shore can only pray are
    safe enough.
I probably sound like a father.

May 1990

Charles C. Finn

In The Whole Wide World

Adam couldn't sleep for feeling punky
so bundling up snug in the rocker we whispered
    about the rain
and rocked in the comfort of the night.
Some moments you know with a certitude
you're at the exact right place
at the exact right time
in the whole wide world,
and this evening I knew.

May 1990

I Cringe To Imagine

On returning from the basement, I met April with tears streaming.
"I couldn't find you anywhere, so I ran out to see if the car
    was gone."
Soon she was soothed and the day resumed its ordinary tenderness,
but the panic of abandonment across her face stays with me.
What about kids, I cringe to imagine, who find the car gone?

June 1990

He's MY Daddy

A boy we met in the video store must have seemed to glance at me
    covetously
for Adam fairly shouted, "He's *my* Daddy!"
leaving the boy speechless,
his mother smiling,
Adam satisfied with his emphatic style,
and me secretly pleased to be the object of such fierce possession.

June 1990

In The Whole Entire World

"Sometimes you give me things and sometimes you don't.
It's just right.
I wouldn't have any other daddy in the whole entire world."
April's summation of her satisfaction with me
    (uncoincidentally coming after a surprise treat)
spread beaming through my every corpuscle.
Oh, we have our difficult moments,
but most are suffused with tenderness,
bubbling with fun,
inexpressibly sweet.
I wouldn't want any other daughter in the whole entire
    world.

June 1990

261

Taken For Granted

"Daddy, bring me water!"
I didn't appreciate the imperious tone—
2-year-olds in the middle of the night aren't into polite requesting—
but the heat helped me empathize
and I took pleasure in collaborating with water to slake his thirst.
But what pleased me most was the satisfied way
he plopped back down and went promptly to sleep.
No call for thank-you fanfare—
needed Daddy,
Daddy came.
That in the middle of night he can take his father for granted
makes his father's heart sing.

July 1990

At The Carnival

Three highlights at the carnival:
a rhapsodic lecture about the graduates of Croaker College
followed by a daredevil frog-leap;
a clown insulting ball-throwers
until a bulls-eye dumped him sputtering;
a gratuitous kindness by the Age-Guessing Expert in concealing his
    correct written guess
to allow April the ecstasy of a prize.
Far more fascinating for me are the people
than the rides at the carnival.

July 1990

Of Her Honesty And Vision

"You shouldn't have squashed that bug, Daddy,
he's a part of the Earth."
I could have quickly dismissed it,
justified the action for Adam's sake,
scoffed that it was just a nuisance bug,
reinforced the general conditioning,
but in fact she was right.
I didn't *need* to squash it,
was in the process of sweeping it towards the window
when it faltered within thumb reach and on instinct I squashed it.
I'm glad I canned the nuisance bug sermon,
congratulated her instead on her sensitive perception,
promised to try harder to remember the Earth.
I sing of her honesty and vision.

August 1990

Stampeding Fears

The cross-town drive every parent dreads.
You try to calm wild thoughts, rein in stampeding
    fears,
as you hurry towards the hospital ER
where the message said your daughter had been taken
    after her fall in the park.
Thank God for the final words of the message, "She's
    conscious and clear."
That helped calm the wildest.

August 1990

Yet So Helpless

It's hard seeing any part of a perfect body broken,
particularly if the perfection fractured
is no angel less on Earth than one's daughter.
So strong is love yet so helpless.

August 1990

A Crucible To Come

Adam's partiality to Penny hurts
until I remember the normalcy and the need.
I cheer his good fortune
in having her be for him
what I now can't.
His and my bond remains to be forged
in the crucible to come.

August 1990

We Did It Right

Awakening to thunder she found me on the porch swing
immersed in the storm's approach.
We did it right—
cozied under the Irish blanket,
counted seconds from flash to boom,
talked of many things silly and earnest,
all the while rocking to the rain,
bracing for the climactic, gigantic boom
thankfully that never came.
No sooner had I tucked her back in
and started to write "awakening to thunder"
than back she pattered smiling,
"Daddy, could you write a poem
about me and you and the thunderstorm?"
Smiling back I answer full-hearted,
"I've already started."

August 1990

To What's Basic

I have a choice.
I can look at my daughter's broken arm
and weep for her discomfort and disappointment,
for her loss and grieving,
and even curse at a happenstance so cruel to a vulnerable girl of 6,
or thanks to the accident I can leap to the realization
that she still radiantly is,
that she could have fallen on her head
and had consciousness dimmed or life extinguished
but that the resplendent presence of her instead
still radiantly is!
Accidents can call us home if we let them
to what's basic.

September 1990

It'll Take More Than Piecemeal Prayer

I've serious spirit-work to do.
I try not to be angry much less punitive towards Adam for his
    slowness to potty train,
but even after piecemeal prayer sometimes I uncontrollably am.
What long-forgotten rage boils into such fierce impatience?
Oh, I could easily rationalize it since it doesn't qualify as abuse,
in fact probably comes close to the norm,
but if so pity the norm.
What shaming must it be teaching him, this vitality I call my son,
for me to raise my voice,
express disappointment,
squeeze unkindly?
Exorcising this demon will take more than piecemeal prayer.

September 1990

A Passing Grace

As soon as I entered the door April handed me a note
(everyone else had received theirs already):
"I LOVE YOU DAD."
Just a passing grace from a girl to her father
to make his day.

September 1990

I Did It!

"I did it!"
Nothing more staunch or endearing
could have sounded out from his sleep
to bear witness he's beginning to bask
in the achievement of his two-year-old task.

September 1990

Opportunity To Entrance

I loved the opportunity the shooting star gave me
to entrance April with lyrical facts about our luminous
    atmosphere—
shield against bombardment,
filter against rays,
blanket of insulation,
conductor of rain magic,
membrane around the life of us breathing.
I trust she heard interlaced with the lyricism
the affection.

September 1990

Pilgrimage

Peeing just like Daddy,
watching turds sink like torpedoes,
holding tight or letting go--
it's a very big deal for Adam to have an exciting new arena
    wherein to exert CONTROL.
The exasperation for all concerned
hugely (I strain to remember) is worth it
because of the advance it represents towards the Mecca of
    autonomy.
Pilgrimages, I find comfort in remembering, are never easy.

September 1990

Vitality Flashes Out Fire

"I HATE you!"
"DUMMY!"
Hearing 6-year-old and 2-year-old hurl at each other
    their worst
brings a smile to their father
even as he hovers to insure against violence
if not to mediate resolution.
Vitality flashes out fire—
pray God it's never extinguished
in these fiery gifts of fathomless worth
from the fiery vitality called Earth.

September 1990

Tooth Fairy Panic

The tooth fairy last night just about blew it.
Just as April was waking this morning,
she groggily began reaching under her pillow.
Remembering in a cringing flash,
I quickly slip out the envelope,
tell her to close eyes and count to 20,
then dash in a frenzy to my 50-cent-piece stash
swapping two for the tooth on the run
and barely making it back by 19
for the quick slip back under the pillow.
That she went along with the ruse gives me clues
that neither a cherished belief nor pieces of silver
is she yet ready to lose.

October 1990

A Boost

To give April a boost to make it through the night
    without a diaper,
I rouse her gently before I retire
and carry her in to the potty.
She seldom wakes to the point of coherence,
but over communication I'll take communion any day.
The reward for my service?
The infinity of her trust
and her pride in the morning to be dry.

October 1990

Pure Treat

Our trick or treating tonight was pure treat.
There's no better way to socialize with neighbors
than when children's glee and greed are the focus
    on a friendly Halloween visit.
Tonight it was Witch and Pig
who even when forgetting to cackle or oink
were undiluted hits.
It helps parents sometimes, dulled by routine's tedium,
to see their kids the way the neighbors do,
be captured anew by the beauty and fun of their own
    children's innocence.
Pity those decrying Halloween.

October 1990

Comforting Closure

My current bedtime ritual with April
has me singing her favorite lullaby,
chanting AUM and Kyrie,
then getting more spontaneous.
First she, then I, give voice to whatever comes to mind
    for which we feel grateful.
Depending on our fatigue this can get lengthy.
Finally, I sing a "Heart Song"
where I address the heart of a natural wonder,
like tree or wind or moon or stone,
with words from my own.
Comforting closure to miracle day
before final hug from angel daughter.
Amen.

November 1990

Learning The Fundamentals

When it's April's turn in our night prayer
to tell God what she's thankful for,
she usually starts with heart and lungs,
expands to family and events of the day,
seldom leaves out the atmosphere,
and always ends with the Big Bang
which she happens to think is a very fine name
for the Universe's birth.
Now here's a girl, I'm pleased to say,
who's learning the fundamentals.

November 1990

No More Potent Gift

If a child past the diaper stage keeps wetting the bed,
parents have a spirit-challenge not to shame.
My grandmother remembers wistfully
a full century after the fact
how afraid at 5 she felt in the night
of the morning scolding if her bed were wet.
Parents need strong prayer,
against the strength of punitive instincts buried,
to detach here,
be patient here,
comfort here.
No more potent gift to a child
than acceptance in place of shame.

November 1990

Shared Affection

Adam and I have a tree we hug,
a great white oak we call Gandalf.
Up by the gate we visit it often while waiting for April's bus,
wonder at its full century of living,
admire its rugged girth and majestic spread,
talk to it as to a wise grandfather,
wrap arms around it as far as they reach.
A bond deepens between my son and me
from shared affection for a wizard tree.

November 1990

A Wonderful Clue

April told Penny today how pleased she was
that her parents were good at different things—
a wonderful clue that whatever our flaws
we're modeling a relationship of combined strengths,
hopefully giving her reason to believe it possible
when it comes her time to start looking.

November 1990

And Why?

"Who would do that, and why?"—
April's response after we had explained
that the baby in the front page picture
had been found in a trash bin barely alive.
How parents respond to evil will be remembered.
We talked some about desperation,
about fear that can reach all the way to panic,
about the possibility of intoxication blotting out
    elemental judgment,
but in the end we could only join in her shudder.
Who could leave a newborn in a trash can to die,
and why?

December 1990

Answering The Call For War

A sidewalk vendor the other night,
as we walked through the Market with candles and signs,
spat out with venomous lash, "Trash, trash, trash."
I prepared to have a little talk with my kids
since they had never heard anybody called trash,
much less themselves,
but for concentrating on keeping their candles lit
they hadn't even heard it.
So I postponed for a time my little talk
about what fear and ignorance can turn good people into,
about the need for kindness no matter what,
about the sacrifice to be made without cease
to answer, on behalf of Earth,
call for war with cry for peace.

December 1990

It's A Tricky Thing Imparting Values

"All we are saying
is give peace a chance."
Off and on since the vigil, April has been singing this.
It speaks to her even at 6.
Not that she comprehends the current international   crisis,
but she does seem to fathom that peace hasn't a prayer
unless given a chance.
It's a tricky thing imparting values.
When does it cross over into indoctrination?
I want my children to see that being human
means holding strong enough convictions to give voice to, be ready
to act on,
so, far from hiding my enthusiasms and concerns, I want to share
them.
Not to, I believe to my core, would deprive them of more.
The trick is not to pressure them to join in,
in the giving voice or acting on,
unless they choose to.
Great is a father's joy
when on a matter to him of such import
as awakening the nation from its patriotic trance
he finds his daughter as inclined as he
to give peace a chance.

December 1990

Foundation To Build Their Lives On

My family each winter is exceedingly privileged
to have Grandfather come stay with us.
It's hard to find words for all he provides:
living proof of dignity in aging,
unconditional caring beyond what parents can give,
long ago tales of Penny and the farm,
hundreds of songs at the piano played and sung by heart,
gentle humor and down-to-Earth wisdom
    that grandchildren would suffer for never hearing.
When April and Adam spend hour on end with him,
whether sitting in lap or walking hand in hand,
let's just say they're receiving the foundation of an
    education
they'll build the rest of their lives on.

December 1990

Keeping Faith With The Past

April of the gleaming eyes
gave me the tall task before slipping into sleep
to write a poem about no less immensity
than our newly standing Christmas tree.
What seem to dance at the chance to whisper ancient meaning
are still living spirits of Druids.
It seems they've schemed the whole thing up for our
    psyches' sake—
making once a year holy for the remembering
by gathering kin by blood or spirit around a tree
    emblazoned with light;
making it a giving tree under whose boughs raised in praise
wrapped presents make magic;
making it a birthing tree bowing through darkest night
    over a child's breathtaking light;
making it the symbol tree of all life—
rooted in low Earth, reaching for high heaven.
It speaks hope at the year's most hallowed time
that humans keep faith with their past
by worshipping, consciously or not, their Christmas tree.
Daughter of the gleaming Sun, who knows maybe born-
    again Druid,
this one's for you.

December 1990

Would That They Paid Heed

"Will the war still be when I grow up?"
I quickly reassured her it'll be over long before then,
and besides it's far away and all of us are safe.
This will bear repeating for her fear is real.
It gets me somberly thinking
about 6-year-olds in Israel this very moment
putting on frightening gas masks as sirens make each
    night a nightmare,
and about terrified 6-year-old Iraqis
under unrelenting bombardment and bereavement past
    my capacity to conceive.
The fear my heart couldn't tell my daughter
is that after this insane war's over
there's likely the way the world goes
insanely to be another.
Would that those scheming for war
paid heed to 6-year-olds.

February 1991

Difficult To Answer

"Are we winning the war?"
Simple answer: Soundly.
We control the air,
have inflicted great damage,
but it looks like ground war will be needed to mop up.
Complex answer: In war nobody wins
except vested interests that stand to profit.
Winning militarily can be losing morally
if the motive at root beyond protecting oil
is the need to avenge past humiliation.
It's a question difficult to answer
when the questioner is your 6-year-old daughter
and for starters you're having trouble with the "we."

February 1991

At The Wishing Pond

A handful of pennies
becomes magic for children before a wishing pond.
I gave April and Adam four each,
telling them to be sure before each throw to make a wish.
I'm not sure Adam at 3 could grasp the wish part,
but eagerly he pitched and watched sink,
enamored, it seemed, both of the ritual of it
and of all those coins on the bottom.
April thought long before each toss, then came back subdued.
"My first wish, Daddy, was for the war to end,
the second for the men to come home safely,
the third for no more children to be dead.
The last is a secret."
Heart filled with more than I could find words for,
"Those were beautiful, April," was all I could manage.

February 1991

Adding Shame To His Fear

Counselors need to watch for countertransference,
their own stuff cropping up and getting in the way.
So do parents.
I'm aware of anger coming from somewhere
when Adam keeps saying "I can't!"
I even shook him today when he kept saying it,
adding (I cringe to think it) shame to his fear.
Until I find the courage to name my own shame,
remember its source,
bring it from darkness into the painful but freeing light
    of awareness,
I'll not for unfinished grieving
be able to comfort my son with acceptance
and then to encourage him gently to believe
that like the Little Blue Engine who could
he too can!

March 1991

Rooted Much Further Back

My eruptions of impatience when Adam repeatedly
    says "I can't"
are rooted not in this child here with his transparent fear
but much further back in another child
who cringed knowing the shame of not believing he could.
Over the years he's tried to forget,
but when his son touches a nerve, opens a hidden page,
for dimly remembering he flashes to rage.
Ah, if I can be but brave enough to begin to mourn my
    long ago loss,
then freed at last I can offer my son
the understanding and reassurance he needs
when eloquently he speaks through 3-year-old tears
of our common fears.

March 1991

Somber Reverent, Hearts Touching

I hadn't planned to talk with April about Easter,
but a baby hamster's unexpected demise
made suddenly an occasion.
She suggested we bury it where we buried the fish last year,
and we did.
She asked that I say a prayer at the grave,
and I did.
Softly I thanked the baby hamster
for coming to visit a spell and for bringing us joy,
told him it made us sad he wouldn't grow up
but happy knowing he was returning
flesh and spirit to enrich the Earth.
It was somber between us there at that grave—
somber reverent, hearts touching.
Then April, adding a prayer of her own,
patted the ground and said goodbye,
wished the Earth to be rich but no more baby hamsters to die.
There are different ways of talking about Easter.

March 1991

Hamster Heaven

For the fun and the tenderness,
6 is a perfect age for raising hamsters.
April's sad farewell to the babies
was rapidly offset by two joyful discoveries:
four *new* babies
and a bonanza from the pet shop of three dollars for each!
Not that she's in it for the money,
but at the rate Silky and Spiky are producing
she's got to find a home for them somewhere, right,
why not make a buck for each in the process,
(or a thrilling *three*)?

April 1991

Magical Space

April and I struck it rich.
We halted our baseball game yesterday long enough
    to find eight 4-leaf clovers
and then incredibly this morning found 18 more!
I tell her it just could be our yard is magic
which makes it feel important just standing there
amidst benevolent trees and singing flowers,
frisking dogs and lounging cats,
sand box with shovels and buckets,
ladder and slide and bars for monkey swinging,
sloping hill and garden of plenty,
and now a 4-leaf clover paradise!
Add to it holy ground
where two kids squeal around the bases after smacking
    it past a sprawling daddy
and you've a magical space if ever there was
to live a dream on.

April 1991

Flowing With The Swift Current

I'm learning Grandfather's secret:
he flows with Adam.
If Adam wants to play cards or cut up paper,
if he wants to look at a book,
check things out downstairs,
go for a walk,
or just sit in his lap and chat,
Grandfather just goes with it,
flows with the swift current of a 3-year-old
who loves few things more than time
with his Grandfather who flows.

April 1991

Conjecturing

"Look! There's Adam and there's me, there's two of us"—
my son's evocative exclamation
upon spying in a mystifying mirror
evidence of his binary self or alter ego.
It's curious and a little sad conjecturing what he will lose
when he discovers "Adam and me" are no longer two.

April 1991

For God And Wonnerful Day

The most touching time in our prayer at night
is when each ad-libs to God a litany of thank-you's for the day.
April and I tend to take poetic flight—
from interior wonders like heart and lungs
to the small family of Finn
(including Grandmother and Grandfather and of course the dogs and
    cats and hamsters)
then out to the great family of Earth and the Milky Way
(including Grandmother Star for dying to give us birth)
and finally all the way back to the Big Bang's beginning
(April's favorite place to end).
Adam, not inconsistent with 3, is much more concrete.
After thanking God "for God and wonnerful day,"
he names everything in the room his eyes fall on
until Daddy feels that's enough for one prayer.
I have to believe the Great Mysterious permeating the
    universe
experiences something akin to a swelling of the heart
to hear Earth children drowsily say:
thanks for hamsters and the Big Bang,
thanks for God and wonnerful day.

May 1991

299

Mountain Of Bliss

A truckload of topsoil makes for a great mountain.
While Penny and I are busy with the garden and lawn,
April and Adam play on it for hours—
creative ways up,
paths for sliding down,
tiptop for climber's cry of ecstasy,
barefoot indescribable bliss.
But o the dismay when daddy keeps diminishing it,
carting off load after load to follow *his* bliss—
three new flowerbeds
and bushes and trees that some day too will flower!
Songs could be sung a thousand years by children and
    daddies alike
for a mountain of topsoil bliss!

May 1991

With No One But You, Girl

Can it really be 14 already?
The first seven carried us from magic Chicago
through widening travels and enduring friendships
to the land and house of our dreams
in preparation for a diamond child coming.
The second seven saw come from afar
not one but two diamond children
and lives so filled with parenting partnership
that words can point, perhaps, but never reach.
With no one but you, girl, could it have been so rich
    and so sweet.
Let's plunge into 14 more on our way to 64.

May 21, 1991

Garden Readied For Seed

These are extraordinary times—
my daughter has learned to read!
Treat it not lightly.
Just because it's what typically happens somewhere around age 6
doesn't make it less astounding for this particular girl
whose narrow homebound world is now opening to the galaxies!
It's not just that now she can, she *hungers* to,
keeps five books close at hand as I smile to understand.
First grade will always shine
as the year April's garden was readied for seed—
she learned to read!
In the grand scheme of a life's unfolding, whether the
    scale is cosmic or human,
there is mostly incremental advancing
until, at thundering threshold moments, a rare
    prodigious leap!

May 1991

Beginning The Climb

My kids just finished at their friend's church a week-
    long Bible Camp,
giving me some things to work through.
I want them to learn stories of all religions,
not be restricted to just one,
which makes me uneasy figuring they likely heard say
this is the best book pointing to the best way.
I trust, though, other things we've told them about,
plan on exposing them to,
will help see them metaphorically through.
With a mountain to learn about Jesus,
Bible Camp is as good a place as any
to begin the invigorating climb.

June 1991

A Time For Just Presence

After distraction schemes had failed
and April still couldn't keep from thinking about a scary
    scene in *Watership Down*,
she requested I stay till she fell asleep,
bring my poetry in if I wanted but just sit near.
Deciding this wasn't the time for poetry,
not, at least, the kind with words,
I savored in the darkness the fullness
of living up to the trust of my child,
of easing her fears in the night
with all she needed, my presence.

June 1991

Happy Little Pilot

Cars fascinate my son,
not to mention trucks, tractors and trains,
bikes, buses and planes.
If it moves, it holds him, calls to him,
sets his eyes dancing, his heart prancing.
He loves to climb in my lap near home,
hang out far as I'll let him to glee in the wind or watch
    the wheels spin,
then steer for a stretch by himself with Daddy's hand
    poised to steady.
There's a happy little pilot when we shout our hooray
for navigating us safely home.
It not only moved but he moved it!

June 1991

A Touch Of Both Somehow

I'm not sure whose joy is greater, April's or Penny's.
April's thrill rises to a peak—
barely 7 and learning to ride the magic of a horse!
But Penny's, I have to believe, is wider.
Bareback girl all her country childhood,
now she returns to learn how with a saddle,
not only enjoying up close April's effervescence but remembering
    her own!
Reliving one's childhood can be torture or tonic,
but when what's relived is bursting-with-bliss happy,
then it's unmitigated tonic.
Thrilling for April,
tonic for Penny,
a touch of both somehow
for a saddled heart cherishing them both.

July 1991

A Kind Of Ritual

April just called to say she's homesick
and would I come get her?
What she really wanted was reassuring
not only that she's dearly loved
but that she'll make it fine if she just gives it a chance.
She agreed to call first thing after breakfast if she still
    wants me to come,
but we both know life will likely look brighter by
    breakfast.
It's a kind of ritual to call your daddy
so that each can be reassured.

July 1991

The Light Stays On

Adam had escalated his late night commotion—
agitating his sister trying to sleep—
to the point where Penny warned him to stop
or else the light would go off.
After a brief silence came the plaintive reply:
"Is that so the monsters can get me?"
"There aren't any monsters," came her wise response.
"Mommy and Daddy won't ever let anything get you."
End of commotion.
Henceforward we'll find a different consequence—
the light stays on.

July 1991

She's On To Something Real

April's thoughts turn often to death.
Enough baby hamsters have died
that she doesn't want any more pets, period,
fearing they too would die.
And off and on since Penny's brief choking, she says
    she has this awful fear
thinking of mommy and me and wondering what if?
She's on to something so real that I don't want to steer
    her away,
but I don't want her to get stuck here either.
I find myself saying that I feel these things too sometimes
    because death is a real hard one,
but we just have to trust things to God and Earth
and in the meantime savor this magic called life.
No intellectual resolution, to be sure,
but it's a comfort to us both, I think,
to find we can give voice to fear without giving in to it,
can in fact let it remind us of magic.

August 1991

A Jungian All Of 7

After being scared by something in a movie,
April feared she'd dream of a monster coming to eat her.
Penny encouraged her to imagine the monster
and tell it like in the *Three Billygoats Gruff*
to wait for her juicier big sister.
But April didn't want to tell a lie (not having a big sister),
so they brainstormed further
till she came up herself with just the right plan.
"If the monster comes I'll offer it ice cream
and then it'll be my friend and protect me."
Armed now against the deep,
a Jungian all of 7 was ready for sleep.

August 1991

On Sin And Redemption

Sin may not be in vogue, but I've just committed one.
I was so intent on April catching the idea
that I was impatient with Adam's interruptions.
Here I was reading a book to my kids about God,
but by pushing my own agenda,
the last thing I teach by my impatience is anything
    even resembling God.
Ah, but immediately springs hope for redemption.
Tomorrow I'll read it again to Adam, just him and me,
and if for all his questions and digressions we don't get
    past page two,
well, so what if justice isn't done to the book
if it's done to both God and Adam.

September 1991

Awash With Importance

You feel good as a parent when you do it right.
Adam got the emphatic message today
that he's so important he has his own day
when he receives gifts all wrapped up
and cake blazing with candles.
How grand that the people grounding your existence
rejoice in your birth and make you feel special.
When a child awash with importance
succumbs at last to sleep on his birthday night,
his parents, too, succumb restfully
assured in their hearts they did it right.

September 1991

Miraculous Story

"Let me tell you a story.
First there was nothing and then there was something.
Then there was a little something that became a big
    something.
Then the big something became human beings.
The end."
My heart leapt to hear the miraculous story of the
    universe
in the nutshell of a child's innocence.
The only flaw in my daughter's story
is that it hasn't ended.

September 1991

Differential Responses

Multiple emotions flooded me as I listened today
to three I love respond differentially to death.
Penny and April in the back of the van took turns
    reading a horse story aloud
while Adam contentedly played with a new truck.
But then the horse April loved the length of the book
    died and it crushed her.
Thank goodness for her mommy's reassuring words,
    comforting arms.
Adam, curious as to tears and talk of death,
kept asking in 4-year-old non-comprehension,
"Why did he die? Why did he die?"
From wisdom born of fire, Penny soothed the one,
then responded to the other about death that must come
enhancing life that is.
Grief, puzzlement, acceptance
hallowed today the crossing of Virginia.

September 1991

Its Price In Tears

April's sobbing in the van today at the death of King of the Wind
reminds me of her solicitude when but 1
over a butterfly dead on the ground.
I intuited then that her feeling heart
for all the joy and richness it would bring her
would exact its price in tears
down the coming solicitous years.

September 1991

One Bright And Shining

Some children's books scintillate.
I've just discovered one bright and shining—*What Is God?*
    by Etan Boritzer—
and have already read it to April and Adam.
It scintillates because it dignifies both the greatest question
and widely divergent yet secretly kin answers across Earth.
How refreshing to read a book on God
that instead of pushing one parochial view
honors *every* view.
What an affirming respectful message for children to take to
    heart—
that curiosity about the Mystery behind existence
is shared by humans everywhere,
that life's boldest challenge and richest meaning
is not to find the one and only true answer
but to come to one's *own* answer
and then endeavor (no small matter) to live it.

September 1991

Tender Elf

When at last it arrived—
the magical shopping day with her cousin Karen
for which she had been saving for months—
April bought one gift for herself
and then surprise gifts for all the kids at the reunion.
Touched deeply, as much by her joy as her generosity,
I was able to squelch, "Why not more for yourself?"
in favor of, "I cherish you, tender elf."

September 1991

Charles C. Finn

They Should Call A Museum A Church

Little compares with the expansion within a parent
being led by the hand of her or his child
through room after room of relics from Earth.
They should call a museum a church
for its hushed invitation to reverence
before stupendous evolutionary Presence!

October 1991

The Magic Is Passed On

April (apparently out of the blue, but then Christmas is coming):
"Mom, do grown-ups sometimes hide eggs for the Easter Bunny?"
Penny: "Yes, sometimes they do."
April: "Is there really an Easter Bunny?"
Penny: "It depends on what you believe."
April (grinning): "I won't tell Adam."
A young girl is in transition here
without trauma, dishonesty, or injustice to her spirit's hunger.
Instead of magic diminishing,
to beneficiary called little brother now it's passed on.

November 1991

When Cute And Innocent Conspire

The epithet Adam delights to hurl
when aiming for silly effect
is "Doo-Doo Head."
I tell him that's not exactly polite
even if meant friendly,
but not wishing to reinforce
I've been attempting to ignore.
Alas that it can't last longer, this time of grace,
when cute and innocent conspire to make possible
calling people shithead to their face.

November 1991

Salute To King Of The Wind

I've just been commissioned by April
to write a poem about a horse named King Of The Wind
that makes her eyes dance.
I asked if she meant the one in the book,
but she said not exactly.
I asked if that's what she's calling Natar, her riding lesson pony,
but she says no he doesn't go fast enough.
Something then distracted us and now she's asleep.
So all I have to go on
is she wants me to write about a magnificent dream horse
who carries her so swift and free it makes her eyes dance.
I salute you, King Of The Wind.
I celebrate your cherished existence in the expanding heart
    of no less person on Earth than my crystalline daughter
whose hunger for beauty is so fed by you,
whose longing for transcendence is so ignited by you,
that her daddy's eyes, too, are now dancing.

November 1991

Parents Have Their Work Cut Out

Today we were tested.
April performed well in her first horseshow but
    nonetheless came in last.
Secretly hoping for a blue, her disappointment was
    palpable.
We congratulated her from our hearts
for looking so splendid up there and doing her very best
and hoped she believed our eyes as our words
that this day was a success.
So pervasive, though, the pressure to win
that parents to be heard over the cultural shout
have their work cut out.

November 1991

Interlaced In A Loving

"Daddy, write a poem about Husky and Potato, and
    me being gone"—
instructions over the phone from my daughter,
so I have to try.
When packing for the sleepover at Beth's,
she remembered every one of the nonessentials
but forgot Husky and Potato.
You have to understand this is serious.
Husky as his name suggests is her soft brother-to-the-
    white-wolf night companion
loved nearly her entire life.
Adults have only to remember the strength of a like
    affection.
Now Potato is actually a pear, furry prize daddy won at
    a carnival,
but out of whimsy she called it Potato
and we've giggled nightly since.
Husky under one arm, Potato under the other,
interlaced in a loving have been each night all three.
Ah, but not tonight,
so she calls and asks daddy to write a poem about her
    friends
with her being gone.

November 1991

323

Dream House

Among pictures April brought home from school
we found one entitled "Dream House,"
featuring a separate house for herself with the door padlocked,
and, ice cream cone in one hand and key in the other,
her looking out a window smiling.
A rainbow rope over a connecting swimming pool links her house
    to the one next door
where looking out from a window of their own
Dad, Mom and Adam too are smiling.
I'd say we have here a 7-year-old who wants to stay amicably close
but is ready not only for separation but for privacy.
It was heartening to see all the smiles.

November 1991

Heart Of Santa

On Christmas Eve we do the only sensible thing—
bake a cake for birthday Jesus.
Adam's idea last year, it already has the feel of a tradition.
Within the heart of a boy of 4 beats the heart of Santa.

December 1991

That's Not A Problem, Mom

Penny (after seeing April's very long Christmas list):
"That many presents would cost an awful lot of money."
April: "Mom, Santa doesn't have to worry about money,
    he makes the presents."
Penny: "Well, if he takes all those in his sleigh,
he won't have room for all the other kids' presents."
April: "That's not a problem, Mom.
Don't you know that Santa's sleigh is infinite?"
The moral of the story
is that parents are in for an interesting time
if their child still believes in Santa Claus
and can fathom the concept of infinity.

December 1991

Two Celebrations Each Year

Our kids each have an Arrival Day celebration
when they receive a cake and a present on the anniversary
of their half circling Earth to find home.
Tomorrow is April's 7th,
while at the end of March will be Adam's 3rd.
We still celebrate with flair their birthdays,
but thanks to these literal gifts from the blue,
let's just say each year they have two.

January 1992

Nostalgia Doesn't Do Justice

Nostalgia doesn't do justice,
connotes something sentimental and wistful,
pining for long ago and far away.
I prefer celebration of heart, savoring of soul,
in the holiness of remembrance.
Seven years ago tomorrow
Penny and I in unlikely airport sanctuary
first beheld April breathlessly, held April breathlessly.
It stirs deeper than nostalgia each anniversary to remember.

January 31, 1992

Crumpled

I cringe to imagine.
Adam was indignant today
to find one of his drawings wadded up in the wastebasket.
He hadn't said to save it so I didn't,
but it strikes with guilty clarity to realize
he likely remembered me saving some of April's
    when seeing his own pitched.
Thankfully he wasn't too depressed to be mad,
but I cringe to imagine his 4-year-old spirit
momentarily crumpled.

January 1992

Grandfather's Back!

Grandfather's back!
There's little to compare with the joy in very young hearts
when their grandfather of a strong attachment
unseen for long months
comes gloriously back for an extended visit.
There's little to compare with the pleasure brimming a
    seasoned heart
when wherever he goes there are grandchildren waiting
    to cherish his coming.
There's little to compare with the satisfaction in a father's soul
to have a wise, respectful, kindly presence
back not only to grace his home
but to delight the hearts of his children.
Grandfather's back!

February 1992

My Bottom's Burping

Adam with surprised look after passing gas:
"My bottom's burping!"
One of the undiluted joys of parenthood
is when cute sparkles into creative.

February 1992

On The Brink

I've never much been drawn to horses.
Raised in the city I never even saw them up close,
    much less rode one.
I'd watch the Kentucky Derby and that was about it.
On that count alone, no doubt, a deprived childhood.
But destiny has sweetly been known not to be deterred
    by deprived childhoods.
Married to a lifelong horse lover
plus now having a daughter whose eyes dance just to see one
has left little doubt it was just a matter of time
when the destined initiation would begin.
Like within a week!
We went and did it, bought a pinto pony April's
    already named Spirit
who will be brought to our Unicorn Valley
just as soon as the pasture is fenced.
So here I am at the ripe age of 50
standing on who knows what new adventuresome brink
secretly hoping my eyes too might begin
to dance just to see one.

March 1992

For The Sake Of Her Dream

Widespread killing is necessary when clearing a pasture.
It doesn't seem right somehow
that so many young trees should die
for the sake of a horse grazing,
but if no horse then what dies instead
is my daughter's dream.
For the sake of her dream I'll keep killing,
grateful to the trees for their magnificent gift.

March 1992

Ah, Snowman

Some things are hard to look at squarely.
First of all I invite April to help me build a snowman,
but it's clearly my project and preoccupation so not
    surprisingly she wanders off.
Next I choose to go on building my snowman
when family snowballs gleefully start flying.
Then, oblivious of the cause, I discover April messed up
    the snowman's mouth
and not only let her know I'm angry
but toss enough self-pitying dismay her way at my beloved
    art object ruined
to whack her for good measure with shame.
Good God, first I choose the snowman over her,
then, because she acted on the message, I passive-
    aggressively whack her with shame.
Ah, snowman, standing in the yard, supposedly a symbol
    of winter play,
I messed you up today.

April 1992

334

Hope Born Of Pain

If I can bring myself to remember
the variety of ways today I was non-attentive to my kids
and the friction this unsurprisingly led to,
there's hope born of pain I can rise again
to the dignity of being more than just in name
father.

April 1992

A Glimmer Of A Glimpse

Ah, the nights and days of spring!
Who exudes it more sweetly than hyacinth and forsythia,
redbud and dogwood,
each new leaf greenly leaping?
Who trumpets it more resolutely than birds at dawn,
thunder's releasing,
seeds in hand for miraculous unleashing?
But a glimmer of a glimpse into why
we named our glistening girl April.

April 1992

Reassurances

"If I wake up in the middle of the night, I might need you."
"I don't think you'll have to call again, April.
Just remember Mommy and Daddy are with you in your heart
and that everything will be okay.
I love you, girl."
"I love you, Daddy. Tell Mommy I'm okay."

April 1992

What Proud Joy

First she fell on her face (right over the top of Sysco)
but came out of it thankfully with no more than a
    bloody nose.
Then days later Summertime takes off on her
and she has to cling on for dear life.
It's tough watching your kid take up a hobby
that happens to be risky as hell.
A horse is both powerful and unpredictable,
and loss of control can be fatal.
Part of me wishes she had stayed with gymnastics—
risks there too but not so potentially dire.
Ah, but a wiser part of me blesses her choice,
springing as it clearly does from her soul (I can see it
    on her face).
What proud joy is my daughter's
to be disregarding the danger and discovering the dignity
of riding the majesty of a horse!

May 1992

Worthy Of Her Calling

"Your happy nature,
your love of horses,
your sweet personality,
and your enjoyment of reading"—
what her teacher writes she'll remember
about April in the second grade.
What gift to give a child: affirming her essential shining.
Yet another example of a teacher worthy of her calling.

June 1992

Not Destined To Last

April and Adam conjecturing what the language might be
in a movie we wouldn't let them see:
April: "I bet they say dummy and shut up."
Adam: "Ooh, and maybe even Poo-Poo head."
April (whispering to Penny so Adam couldn't hear):
    "Mommy, do you think they're saying shit?"
Let's call it an innocence not destined to last.

June 1992

If Followed By A Heart To Heart

"You don't love me, you think I'm ugly.
You care more for Adam than you do for me."
The histrionics are so amusing
it'd be easy to smile and dismiss it
as just your typical 8-year-old spout and pout,
but I'm struck instead at the opportunity
to sit down when the dust has settled
and have a heart to heart.
"I know you were feeling those things then,
but do you still feel them now?
And is there anything I might say next time
that could help comfort you when you hurt,
or do you just need space till the storm blows over?"
Hurt feelings can be an opportunity
if followed by a heart to heart.

June 1992

Clouds Setting In

Clouds are setting in.
Becoming 5 and 6 and 7 were thrills.
She wasn't just 4, she was 4 and 2/3rd
then 4 and 3/4th and 4 and 5/6th—
getting to 5 was a very big deal, so too 6 and 7,
yearned for with all that was in her.
Not so getting to 8.
She's let it slip she'd rather be 6 again—
I could carry her more then
and school wouldn't be so hard.
Nothing traumatic here,
just clouds of consciousness setting in.

June 5, 1992

Painful Transition

April is making a painful transition.
For the first time she asked me point blank
if the tooth fairy were really mommy and me.
Before it had been, "Is there really a tooth fairy?"
    which allowed room for truthful evasion,
but today she allowed no evasion.
I suggested she think further before asking me that
because I would be honest in responding,
but she calmly said she wanted to know now, "and be truthful,
    Daddy."
So I was truthful,
but as clue to the pain experienced
her eyes flinched and her lips quivered before she slipped off to her
    room.
Finding her wrapped in her blanket sobbing, I could only try with
    my arms to console her.
"I wish you hadn't told me that, Daddy."
"You made it clear you needed to know, April.
Had I been untruthful to protect your feelings,
think of your hurt later to discover my lie.
There's still magic, girl, but now it's time to learn a different kind:
 keeping it alive for Adam."
I wonder how soon she'll ask me point blank about Santa?

July 1992

343

Astounding Emergence

From *A God Within* by Rene Dubos:
"The human brain is three times as large at six years of age
    as it is at birth,
and its fundamental architecture develops through this early
    period
through an elaborate sprouting of dendrites.
Language, imagination, consciousness and sense of self-
    identity
also reach a high level of development at that time."
Dignity, demand, delight—
all are caught up in the magnitude of the calling
both to witness and to guide this astounding emergence
of a young human life!

July 1992

Loss And Gain

April and I used to have endearing chats,
now we have serious conversations.
It seizes the heart of parents
to witness their children's innocence wane—
ah, but the things they now gain.

July 1992

He Thought He Could

"Why don't I put the training wheels back on, Adam,
        it's just not yet the time."
"No, I want to try again."
While cheering the spirit of this Little Blue Engine,
I feared his dejection if he kept attempting what for the
        time seemed beyond him.
Suddenly I look up and he's doing it—
not, to be sure, without jerks and wobbles,
but my son was riding a bike without training wheels!
We cheered in unison—
he for his proud new skill, I for his undaunted spirit.
He thought he could, he thought he could, he thought he could.

August 1992

What Wise Parents Might Say

A nugget from *The Gospel Of Thomas*:
"Do not lie or do what you dislike."
It's what wise parents might say to their children
    embarking on life:
find honor in honesty
and fiercely follow your star.

August 1992

Spirit-Challenge

A father with pacifist leanings
having a son enamored of the rhetoric of violence
has a spirit-challenge facing him—
how to model less dramatic but dramatically more creative
    solutions to the problems of living
when the cultural drift (not to mention his own buried
    impulses)
incline decidedly towards aggression?

August 1992

Destined From The Start

Take April's enthusiasm after her first lesson,
add to it her teacher's praise of her talent and spirit,
crown it with the significance of the event itself—
piano's grand entry into her life!—
and you have what just could be the beginning
of a relationship destined from the start
to set to dancing not just her fingers but her heart.

September 1992

349

The Best Fortune

"Mystical religion is largely caught—
to be exposed to the kind of adult who has the
    authentic qualities of inwardness and gatheredness,
developed through prayer and contemplation,
is the best fortune that can befall the child."
A comforting reminder from the Quaker John Yungblut
of a gift I may be giving my children.

September 1992

More Than Just Our Reflection

April's third grade class voted today—
Bush 22, Clinton 8.
Rural Virginia doesn't look promising
if kids can be trusted to reflect the views of their parents.
April was forthright in opposing Bush on account of his war
but apparently swayed few.
I like her reasoning and her spunk—
she thinks war is a dumb way to solve problems
and is not afraid to say so.
I'll not deny our influence,
but she's more, I trust, than just our reflection.

September 1992

351

Widening Horizons

A storytellers' convention,
then a powwow two weeks later—
a more than normally rich October.
When we widen the horizons for our children,
I rejoice to believe we're living up
to our extravagant calling.

October 1992

It's Just One Of Those Things

When you trap an escaped hamster in the closet
and in the scramble to catch it have your knee land on
    its head and kill it instead,
you have two choices.
One is lie and say he got away,
a not too traumatic way for the kids to lose their friend.
The other is be truthful—
share what happened, how bad you feel, and ideas for
    a funeral.
Not wishing to live with the guilt of a lie to cover a blunder,
thankfully I opted for the truth.
From April I received a tender hug:
"Now don't feel bad, Daddy, it's just one of those things."
Adam couldn't get over how stiff it was in that baggie
and how its eyes could still be open when it was flat dead.
If they're not giving me a hard time, I think with relief,
    why should I?
Best of all I won't have to try to keep covering a lie.

October 1992

Not Idly Did We Name Her

April and I rehearse each day for the family skit at her
    her school this Friday.
She's the Sun and I'm the North Wind,
and following Aesop's guide we're wagering our pride
on disrobing wayfarers Penny and Adam.
The Sun of course wins this one,
gentle persuasion being smarter than brute force.
She giggles to cue me whenever I forget my lines
and loves to see my extravagant bluster—
it's not often I get a chance to out huff and puff the
    Big Bad Wolf,
alas to no avail.
What I most of all love is the gleam in her eyes,
her sparkling delight beaming warmth and light.
Not idly did we name her Hae Dal,
Korean for Daughter of the Sun.

November 1992

Adding To The Wealth

I got to ham it up tonight—I was the North Wind!
The four of us in hopeful justice to Aesop
did a skit at April's school—
a great chance for families to get creatively silly
and add to the wealth of their memories.
April as the Sun had the chance she's been waiting for—
    to call me a big blow—
and I got to make a blustering spectacle of myself
trying in vain to prove myself the stronger
by blowing off the coats of Penny and Adam.
Then the serene Sun, aptly played by his Daughter,
did her gently persuasive thing and achieved what force
    could never.
Ah, how we added tonight to the wealth of our memories.

November 1992

Daddy, Que Sera!

The final minutes each school morning before leaving
    to get to the bus
are not among our most tranquil.
Much needs doing and fast,
and since the kids are not into worry
Daddy takes it upon himself to hurry.
In the midst of yesterday's flurry, April fixed me with
    a glare,
"Daddy, que s*era*!"
Not wishing at that precise moment to be reminded of
    my philosophy,
I glared back and kept up the fuss.
At least I managed a thanks for the reminder
before she boarded the bus.

November 1992

Solid Grounding

April to Penny: "You're the nicest mom I ever had.
My other mom is nice,
but she probably wouldn't have done all this for me."
How possible a more solid foundation
for a girl adopted in infancy?
While not doubting original loving,
she's convinced of a superabundance of present loving.
Solid grounding for a lifetime to come.

November 1992

Charles C. Finn

What Only Matters

My daughter's taking to piano almost as much as to horses.
But two months of lessons and already she's playing
    Christmas carols
and more important is loving it.
Who knows how far she'll take it,
or it takes her?
What only matters is she's learning by leaps
and loving it!

November 1992

Reality Comes Zinging

"Yes, but sometimes you hurt us when you grab and
    jerk us."
I didn't like hearing it.
Here I was congratulating myself on not spanking
and suddenly reality from my daughter comes zinging.
When fired by anger my touch clearly burns
so until I can extinguish through soul-work the need for
    so many fires,
I'd best not touch when angry.

December 1992

Red-Letter Night

There's the taste of archetypal joy in a bubbling 5-year-old boy
who tonight picked out a beagle puppy
for whom he could think of no more felicitous name
than (because of her curly tail) Piggy Wiggy.
So a cigar to you across time
from a red-letter night in a past December—
our family has a new member!

December 1992

Hearing What She Needs

Receiving with reverence a child's gift
gives said child what she needs:
validation and appreciation.
We just got back a Christmas snapshot
of Penny rapt before a gift of beads
from April holding her breath
to hear what she needs.

January 1993

Daddy, You Said A Bad Word

April heard me hollering in my study
and asked what was wrong.
"Two more piles of dog crap
and *that's* why I don't want her in here at all."
"Daddy, you said a bad word. You said crap."
I slowed down, then heard myself saying,
"You're right, April, that's kind of vulgar.
When you get frustrated, like I am now at Piggy,
you sometimes let things fly.
That was a pretty mild one, actually."
She seemed satisfied and moved on,
hopefully remembering to be acceptant of herself
when someday she too lets things fly.

January 1993

Premonition

Just when I think of reinforcing Adam and his guest
    for playing so well together,
I hear thuds and gleeful cries from the bedroom.
I open the door to see them literally stomping on the
    pinball machine received at Christmas,
smashed now beyond repair.
So much for trusting 5-year-olds to play unattended.
Adam was either trying to impress
or haphazardly following the lead,
neither consoling to his father's premonition
of someday adolescence.

January 1993

Ease Up, Daddy

I'm not enough patient.
My son often responds to even mild challenges with "I can't"
and then not surprisingly doesn't try.
It bothers me enough to get on him about it.
"There you go again, Adam, saying you can't before
　　you even try.
Remember the Little Blue Engine, come on, just do it!"
What may have begun encouragement ends up irritation.
I wonder what a father's disapproval
adds to a boy's insecurity?
I also wonder what memories must get stirred
in the father to be so irritated?
Ease up, Daddy, on yourself as well as him.
Trust the Little Blue Engine in both of you
to pick up steam when there's something to dream
on the other side of the mountain.

February 1993

Unselfconscious Simple And Real

The new boy at preschool kept staring at Adam's face,
kept saying to his father, "What's that?"
Adam, his teacher reports, was baffled,
couldn't figure what the boy meant.
The boy's father was about to intervene
when wise teacher said, "No, they can handle it."
Finally the boy blurted, "Did a cat scratch your face?"
"Oh," was Adam's prompt reply, "that's just my birthmark.
Here, (earnestly rolled up his sleeve) let me show you
     where I *do* have a cat scratch."
We both laughed, Emilie to tell and I to hear
how unselfconsciousness simple and real
turned potential humiliation into no big deal.

March 1993

Sure An' Begorrah

A St. Patties we'll remember.
Before she went to sleep, April and I had poured out
    our sorrow for ourselves and Dromia,
gray tabby gone now in deep snow for six days.
Ah, the purity of shared grieving.
Having experienced that holiness and then tiptoeing out,
who do I hear from the porch and then see at the door
    but Dromia!
In an intoxication that a Guinness can never reach,
scooping him up in my arms I rushed back
to thrill a girl from her sleep.
Sure an' begorrah but it's been a St. Patties
we'll forever in our hearts keep.

March 1993

Trying To Be Matter Of Fact

"Dad, I'm leaking."
"Go tee-tee and then get a towel. No big deal."
I tried to be matter of fact.
He's been without a diaper now for a good week
    and generally doing great.
The wavering spoke fear that maybe it *was* a big deal
and that I'd add disappointment to his own.
I pray he found relief in addition to a towel.

May 1993

Charles C. Finn

Hiking To Nannie's

A bright mid-May day
found Adam and me hiking to Nannie's.
I figured he'd tire and turn at the bridge,
but never bet against 5-year-old determination.
By the time we reached the little store
we had worked up thirst and appetite
so satisfied both.
And we needed a bag of candy of course
to sweeten the return.
Friendly horses and scary dogs,
trusty walking sticks and shiny stones,
bugs and butterflies, creeks and dragonflies,
Virginia creeper and poison ivy,
cars and trucks zooming,
clouds and turkey buzzards drifting—
there's so much to see and chat about
when you journey through the kingdom at hand
in the company of a princely son.

May 1993

Seldom An Outcome So Felicitous

Adam likes to compete and win.
Today it was no contest—
thirteen ticks on him, only one on me.
For a kid usually scared of insects,
with each crawling discovery on our hike
    you should have seen him grin.
Seldom an outcome so felicitous—
I no less joyous to lose than he to win.

May 1993

Double Ripening

Advice on my 16th wedding anniversary to a man
    searching for a wife:
find your lifework first,
your bliss station,
your path with heart.
Doors then will not only open,
life mate will walk through
who, like you for her, has been ripening for you.

May 21, 1993

Your Spirit Lives, Gray Fox

The book, *Gray Fox*, not only touches April's heart,
it opens her soul.
This came through soft and clear when she looked through
    it there in the store,
so despite having declared this was not a buying trip,
of course we bought it.
It's the story of a fox, alive in the beauty of the changing seasons,
finding mate, having cubs, then just like that
struck dead by a car in the night.
There's sadness here but not tragedy
as Gray Fox's spirit lives on in his cubs
who soon are adults seeking mates of their own and then
    having cubs of their own
alive in the beauty of the changing seasons.
Tender affirmation is here
of nature and life,
of beauty and spirit,
of endurance of what matters.
Twenty times I bet she's already read it
for so touching her heart and opening her soul.
Your spirit lives, Gray Fox.

May 1993

Leaping With Gray Fox

April: "He's a lot like you."
Me: "How's that?"
April: "He feels like you do,
for Earth and spirit that never dies."
I had just read to her *Gray Fox*,
not your normal kids' book skirting death.
This one walks right up to it and through it,
leaves you aching for a wonderfully alive fox
killed suddenly by a car at night.
But you're heartened toward healing
first by a sensitive boy who carries him,
who with a prayer then buries him,
then by his cubs who soon have cubs of their own
all wonderfully alive with the spirit of Gray Fox.
When we read about the author on the book jacket
and she told me he's a lot like me,
my soul all at once felt wonderfully alive
leaping with Gray Fox.

May 1993

Distinctions

Chatting with Adam about the adoption picnic,
I commented on how many countries were represented,
    adding "And you were the only one from Hong Kong,"
to which he casually responded,
in a tone combining matter of fact with hint of further
    distinction,
"And mine was the only birthmark."
This led me to tell him about the great symbol on April's
    flag of origin—
the darkness of yin and the brightness of yang—
which danced across his very face.

June 1993

Charles C. Finn

Do Spiders Got Bones?

"Do spiders got bones?"
"No."
"Good."
That was our final brief exchange in the camper
before Adam drifted to sleep.
I guess he figured even if one got it,
it'd be harmless without bones.
It comforts a father's heart
whether in matter grave or slight
to reassure his son in the night.

June 1993

To The Farthest Reach

It carries a man to the farthest reach
to hear his daughter just turned 9
play beloved themes on the piano
that have nourished him down the years.
Today it was *Ode To Joy* and the New World Symphony—
played with verve and skill,
music to a father's ears.

June 1993

On The Merits Of Surrendering One's Agendum

When April informed me the hike was no fun because I was
    so grouchy,
I started on instinct to defend myself but then had the
    wisdom to realize
that this Father's Day adventure had a chance to succeed
only if Daddy surrendered his own agendum
and let his kids take the lead.
What a time we then had for hours,
the three of us in earnest sync
catching minnows in a mountain creek!

June 1993

Two Flattened Snakes And A Cat

We're used to opossums and skunks on the road
splattered and flattened by wheels in the night,
but today it was two snakes and a cat,
the latter being gorged by five buzzards.
Adam wondered if they eat the eyes
and I said probably.
He couldn't get over the blood.
I got to thinking it could have been Dromia
and what then would I think of the buzzards
and where would his tabby spirit then be?
Later Adam dictated a letter to Grandfather,
beginning "I hope you live for hundreds of years."
Here's guessing he too was still thinking
about two flattened snakes and a cat.

June 1993

Three Grieving

April's biological mother not only must remember
    the original piercing
but likely experiences a dull ache since
whenever she allows herself to wonder where and
    how her daughter might be
whom she'll never see.
I grieve for her that she'll never know
the beauty, spirit, and captivating whirl
of the pearl of her precious girl.
April's heart too, when she allows it to,
will know grieving.

July 1993

Anticipating A Possible Test

I wonder sometimes if my kids' way of rebelling
will be to become fundamentalists.
That'd certainly test my philosophy of tolerance,
my trust that people get to where they need to get to
and learn what they need along the way.
Guidelines I'll teach and hope they remember:
Is it really so important what you call it?
Does it call you home to Earth who cries for healing?
Does it teach you to listen respectfully in order to learn
or to demean by trying to convert?
Does it honor truth unfolding, in league with the cosmos
     unfolding,
or insist Truth is fixed forever and woe to those falling
away?
Hmm, if they're going to rebel,
what better way than against their father's guidelines?
Just call it anticipating a possible test.

August 1993

Quandary

Put it to them gently but tell them the truth.
The longer it's concealed, the more tempting to
    keep it concealed,
to lie then to cover evasion.
Not that they'll be able to comprehend suicide,
but then who of us can?
No, shouts a second voice within.
Children, just 9 and near 6, have enough trouble
    grappling with death's finality,
even of a turtle or hamster,
without unnecessary confusion added by mention
    of self-infliction.
Such is a father's quandary returning to his kids
from the funeral of their cousin.

August 1993

A Good Start

Both feel school's off to a good start.
For Adam any day has to be good
that begins with boarding the big yellow bus.
After all those years of waving with Daddy to his
    important big sister,
at last he and she *both* can climb aboard
and this time it's Daddy alone doing the waving.
And his kindergarten teacher is the same April had!
For April pleasure number one is being with Caitlyn again—
there's nothing quite like having a best friend—
and she too is happy with her fourth grade teacher
    who's challenging but fair.
As the bus pulls away in the morning, tugging a little
    at my heart,
it helps knowing they're off to a good start.

September 1993

Maybe I'm Just Better At Burying It

I flash out with anger when he laughs at another's misfortune.
Tonight at dinner when he did it again, I sent him to his room.
Back and forth I battle within
between justifying the needed message that this is unacceptable
and questioning my unnecessary anger,
and wondering, too, if instead of reacting to the negative
I should wait for his generosity to reassert itself
and then make sure to praise.
Hmm, it strikes me as I write,
I've known firsthand, more often than I'm comfortable admitting,
the instinct to laugh at another's bad luck,
so maybe I'm just better than my son at burying it deep under.
Maybe if I can learn to accept and forgive myself,
I can still give him the needed message
but without the anger.

September 1993

Extended Welcome

Adam's most recent one-liner was the other night over dinner:
after we had asked our guests how long they could stay,
he thoughtfully exclaimed: "You can stay with us till you die!"
Have guests ever in the annals of hospitality
received more extended welcome?

September 1993

On The Brink Of Embarking

Assuming all along she'd hit puberty maybe at 11 or 12
ill-prepared me to realize it's starting to happen
and she's only 9.
Part of me weeps at the loss,
part of me exults at the imminent blossoming,
part of me is seized with intimations of seismic shifts
    ahead to shake all of us,
part of me bows before the mystery.
All of me in spite of myself says yes.
This girl on the brink of embarking upon the lovely
    storming sea
for the fabled port called Bearer of Life
is none other (I gasp to conceive)
than my once and only present daughter.

November 1993

Argumentum Ad Senioritatem

When April told Adam in self-assured tone that
    heliocopters were not airplanes,
he suspiciously responded, "How do you know *that*?"
to which came her classic reply, "I just know things,
I've been in the world longer than you."
Hmm, now where do you suppose she's heard that?

December 1993

The Poisoned Spring

Out I staggered, bemoaning desert heat and awful thirst,
and gasped to the wailing wind (and listening audience)
that my fellow prospectors and I would be goners for sure soon
if we didn't find water.
And then I behold the glorious sight—a gurgling spring!
(actually a big yellow pail with a cup of water inside
 nestled carefully amidst the confetti)
The rest you can guess.
I drank ecstatically, clutched my throat dramatically,
then keeled over with great aplomb.
One by one four comrades arrived, aged somewhere
 between 6 and 10,
each proceeding to sweetly taste then croak with a flourish.
Then arrived the second to last who was about to drink
when out burst April yelling POISON
(she claimed the honor for being director of operations)
and then sweeping up the bucket and dashing down from
 the stage
to empty it over gasping spectators.
My only regret was that as the first one dead I couldn't
 watch the fun.
Ah, but the sound to me was music
because the experience was golden
as I lay listening, past the high drama and pure laughter,
to the thunder drumming in the heaving chest
of a proud happy father.

December 1993

Terrified Question

"Are you and Daddy getting a divorce?"
After hearing the heat in our voices,
she put to Penny her terrified question.
Thankfully she could ask it in order to receive reassurance,
but how quick to leap, I muse, and how near
is a child's fear.

January 1994

Already She's Enamored Of Gandalf

It's a joy to be beginning
to be able to share with my mind-burgeoning daughter
books I have come to love.
Today we began *The Hobbit*
and already she's enamored of wizard-to-my-soul Gandalf.
Such a wealth of awakening spirit
to compensate for early childhood receding.
A father laments at the exact same time that he strikes it rich.

January 1994

Pure Artistry

First he takes three plastic straws
and with the help of staples turns them into a huge A—
understandable given his name.
But then inspiration strikes as he staples the legs
into loops just big enough to hold rubber snakes.
Voila, an ingenious snake-carrier
to surpass for pure artistry any poem his father makes.

February 1994

But Never At Grandmother's

Adam is enamored of dirty words.
He loves when I give him permission to utter his worst
    and then giggle.
Bodily functions of course are his favorites but
    anything shocking will do.
Time alone will tell if this strategy backfires,
but I figure why not mix in with good fun a lesson
    about sensitivity to others,
that there's a time and a place
but never at Grandmother's.

April 1994

Privileged To Watch Flower

"What a joy to have had her in my class.
April's one of those sparkling students
I wish I could follow all the way through
just to watch her develop."
It not only made me beam to hear it,
it led as I was driving home
to the realization amounting to a revelation
that Life's amazing grace to Penny and me
is that we *do* get to follow her through.
What an exotic Earth plant
we're privileged to watch flower!

May 1994

The Moody Blues Are Coming!

The Moody Blues are coming!
I hurried when I heard it to get tickets for the four of us
sensing the magnitude of the family event
both to experience and look back on.
The kids have heard our albums enough to be excited at
    the prospect,
and Penny and I reminiscing richly are nothing short of
    thrilled.
You have to understand with the Moody Blues it's not
    just the music,
it's the cosmos breaking through—
hyperbole only to the non-comprehending.
The Moody Blues are coming!

June 1994

Morning Ritual

"Wake me up please so you can cuddle me! OK? April Finn."
A note for Mommy on the tea kettle, so she'd be sure not to miss it.
The morning ritual through the school year,
prior to Penny's early departure,
had the kids and her on the sofa snuggling drowsy and warm.
So comforting the bond, the love-rich easing awake,
that summer's opportunity to sleep late
loses out to a morning ritual
to build not only a day but a life on.

June 1994

Charles C. Finn

Helping A Befuddled Daddy See

"But what if we close the door gently
and then it slams all by itself?"
I had been telling April and Adam about behaviors
    like slamming doors
that could earn them allowance deductions
when Adam with straight face but twinkling eye
tried to help his befuddled daddy see
how unjust it would be to blame an innocent child
for what just might conceivably have been
an errant hefty breeze!

November 1994

Worth His Salt

Let's face it, winning means something.
When two teams face off—
matching skills, strategy and stamina—
the goal is to win.
So of course victory is sweet and defeat disappointing.
But if a coach is worth his salt,
meaning a human being before a coach,
then he teaches that success is more than winning
and failure has nothing to do with defeat.
Though well pleased my daughter's basketball team
    won a robust 9 of 11,
I'm pleased even more about what the team learned
about challenge and effort and teamwork and fun
from a coach who succeeds.

December 1994

I Smiled As I Poured

An exchange to help the day get started:
Daddy: "I didn't put milk in your cheerios yet, Adam.
　　I didn't want them to get soggy."
Adam: "I *want* them to get soggy. My teeth are not
　　awake yet, they need something soft."
Begging pardon of sleepy teeth,
I smiled as I poured.

January 1995

Until Prompted By A Heartfelt Worry

When you live with a woman 19 years
you despair of even trying to catch her living essence in words
until prompted by her heartfelt worry
that a raccoon scurrying from a brush fire
might have left her babies behind.

February 1995

Jacking It Up A Gear

Simultaneous with awe
a shudder rises from me—
my daughter's body buds
(mystery coursing through her)
with the promise of the danger
of the sweetness of life.
Fatherhood courageous and wise
will have to jack it up a gear
to see me through this one.

February 1995

Unless It's All You've Got

Minor league hockey sounds bush league ho-hum
unless it's all you've got.
The kids knew nothing more of hockey
than what they'd seen in *Mighty Ducks,*
but that was enough of a preparation for the real thing.
A win would have been nice in our three games this year,
but then there's next year.
The last one I splurged for box seats to put us close to the action.
April chatted with friends,
Adam cheered the fights,
Daddy just took it all in.
Bush league you can live with if it's all you've got.

April 1995

Glimpse

What April in last night's prayer was thankful for:
"My home,
my friends,
horses,
just life!"
But then something not to be left out:
"And being able to play "The Funeral March."
I smile from my soul
for this glimpse into hers.

January 1997

About The Author

Finn spent ten years in the Society of Jesus after graduating from high school in Cincinnati. With degrees in literature and psychology from Chicago's Loyola University, he taught high school and then became a mental health counselor before relocating to Virginia with his wife in 1979. He lives near Fincastle with his family and commutes to nearby Salem where he is a licensed professional counselor. He has counseled addicts since 1982.

Among Finn's writings is the internationally-known poem "Please Hear What I'm Not Saying." His published works, all of which can be obtained through his website (www.poetrybycharlescfinn.com) or e-mail address (*charlesfinn@ntelos.net*), include the following:

Circle of Grace: In Praise of Months and Seasons
Natural Highs: An Invitation to Wonder
For the Mystically Inclined
Contemplatively Sweet: Slow-Down Poems to Ponder
Earthtalks: Conjectures on the Spirit Journey
The Elixir of Air: Unguessed Gifts of Addiction

All of Finn's writings relate to the spirit journey. His own has been grounded in Catholicism and nourished by Jesuit, Taoist, Native American, Creation-Centered, and Quaker spiritualities.

Printed in the United States
35770LVS00004B/106-153